Profile of a City

Profile of a City

Prepared by Members of the Economics Department
FIRST NATIONAL CITY BANK
New York, N.Y.

Introduction by Nathan Glazer

McGRAW-HILL BOOK COMPANY
New York   St. Louis   San Francisco   Düsseldorf
Kuala Lumpur   London   Mexico   Montreal
New Delhi   Panama   Rio de Janeiro
Singapore   Sydney   Toronto

Library of Congress Cataloging in Publication Data

First National City Bank. Economics Dept.
    Profile of a city.

    1. New York (City)—Economic conditions. 2. New
York (City)—Social conditions. I. First National City
Bank. II. Title.
HC108.N7F57   309.1′747′104   72-8472
ISBN 0-07-021066-7

*The editors for this book were William G. Salo, Jr. and
Ross J. Kepler, the designer was Naomi Auerbach, and its production
was supervised by Stephen J. Boldish. It was set in Plantin by
York Graphic Services, Inc.*

*It was printed by Halliday Lithograph Corporation and bound by
The Book Press.*

1234567890 HDBP 765432

Contents

Preface

A tradition of service to the community that dates back to 1812 explains why a leading financial institution should concern itself with the problems of the community around us. Our interest in compiling these studies was to broaden our own understanding of the forces and influences acting on the area and to contribute what we could toward improving the quality of life. The studies were undertaken by a group of economists organized into a Regional Research Section of our Economics Department. Their mission is to assess metropolitan area problems, evaluate them, consider alternatives, and suggest practical solutions.

A detailed examination of urban affairs raises a number of questions, not the least of which is how the problems confronting the New York metropolitan area reached their present dimensions. This question has particular relevance to other communities since our studies suggest that as a community grows, it must anticipate sharply rising costs of services. A community should, at the same time, expect that its efforts to provide critical services to increasing concentrations of people will precipitate a dismaying range of problems.

In a very real sense, New York City, as the nation's largest urban center, represents the ultimate in urban problems. Therefore, progress made toward amelioration of New York's urban problems has meaning for other communities; such progress may show the way out of a maze. The purpose of this book is to point directions, not fingers;

to suggest solutions, not to cast blame in hopes that our studies will be of use to others concerned about finding ways to allocate our vast national resources to help more Americans attain individual fulfillment.

WILLIAM I. SPENCER

New York, N.Y.

President, First National City Bank
First National City Corporation

Acknowledgments

Profile of a City reflects the concern of First National City Bank as an institution and its employees as citizens for the welfare of New York City. Individual chapters were prepared by members of the bank's Regional Economics Section as indicated below. Their contributions must be viewed within the larger framework of the bank's Economics Department, which is directed by Leif H. Olsen, Senior Vice President and Chief Economist. It is the department's function to study economic conditions broadly and to ascertain directions and trends. These published efforts are part of that function.

Editorial assistance was provided by a number of the bank's economists, especially Harvey H. Segal, Vice President. The authors are grateful to the dozens of people whose contributions range from dredging out elusive facts to shepherding copy.

Metropolis	George P. Roniger Senior Economist
Poverty and Economic Development	Jac Friedgut Vice President and Nathan Bloom Senior Economist

Public Education	Jac Friedgut and Rosalind Landes Assistant Cashier
Housing	Nathan Bloom
Transportation	Nathan Bloom
Environment	Barrett J. Riordan Associate Economist
City Government	George P. Roniger Senior Economist

Introduction

by Nathan Glazer

Professor of Education and Social Structure,
Harvard University

There are three aspects of this group of studies of a great city—New York, at the turn of the seventies—that should make it of the first importance to all of us who are concerned with the future of American cities.

First, despite the exclusive concern in these studies with the problems of New York, the specifics of the New York situation, the figures and numbers of New York, what these essays report is generally true of all large American cities.

It is obvious that the issue of pollution is found in every large city of the United States, and the hard choices affecting how we deal with it—choices between convenience and low cost on the one hand as against a higher standard in the environment on the other—will have to be dealt with everywhere.

It is clear the peculiarly intractable problems of poverty and welfare are to be found almost everywhere. As the welfare population shot up in the second half of the 1960s, there was a common early reaction that something special was going on in New York City: perhaps the rise was due to its distinctive immigration mix of blacks and Puerto Ricans, its special job structure, the liberal government of Mayor Lindsay. Many other special reasons were suggested. Alas, it turned out the explosion in welfare was a national phenomenon, as marked

1

in Mayor Yorty's Los Angeles and in Mayor Daley's Chicago as in New York. And indeed, early in President Nixon's administration it became a national priority to introduce some basic reform into the welfare system.

Education in New York City has some distinctive features: the enormous power of the teachers' union, for example; the special ethnic composition of the teaching force and the higher administrators; the distinctive history of excellence, still carried on by the specialized high schools and perhaps in other parts of the system. But here too, whatever is distinctive about New York City is fast fading in a general national crisis over urban education: its rapidly increasing cost, its inability to show substantial progress in educating the new urban minorities, its loss of authority in the face of challenges from militant communities and rebellious students. These are no longer distinctive New York City problems, if they ever were.

One would think, if anything was uniquely distinctive of New York City, marking it off from all other American cities, it is its housing. New York stands alone among American cities in the very high proportion of its housing stock that is in multiple dwellings and the very high proportion that is rental housing. And for these reasons, it remained the only American city to maintain rent control without a break from World War II until the present. A few years ago a striking phenomenon—one never seen before in any American city, or perhaps in any other cities, since the decline of the urbanism of the ancient world—appeared in New York: the abandonment of sound housing. The suddenness and scale of this phenomenon left all analysts for a while dumbfounded, even if moviemakers rapidly added to their gallery of visual images scenes in the abandoned and burned-out apartment houses in New York, where drug addicts and other down-and-outers might occasionally shelter themselves. It seemed clear to many that rent control explained housing abandonment. The fact is that housing abandonment has now spread to other large cities, with rather different characteristics of housing stock and housing administration. Even here New York is not completely unique.

Alongside the characteristics of its housing stock, the most distinctive feature of New York in contrast to other American cities is its system of mass transportation. The density of family units in large apartment houses and the density of jobs in large office buildings and factory lofts made it economic to provide mass-transportation facilities expensive to build and to maintain, and they survived in New York during a time when in other cities some equivalent facilities were abandoned. The cycle of limited service, less use, less income, and less service was to be found in New York City, too, as ownership and use of the automobile rose, even in the crowded city. But it did not reach the point where, as in Los Angeles, a remarkable system of street railways was completely abandoned. New York's mass transportation survived into a new epoch, one marked by increasing concern over pollution and congestion because of the use of the automobile and increasing concern for amenity as great areas were leveled for freeways. Thus, New York's public transportation system is expanding at the same time as other cities are beginning to build their own. And at this stage in history, it is doubtful whether New York has many special advantages in the maintenance of a public transportation system anymore. All mass transit is increasingly limited to the journey to and from work. And how can these enormously expensive facilities be maintained for maximum use for only a few hours a day? New York is now struggling with the same issues other cities are now pondering—how the mass transit is to be financed, how taxes can be levied on users of automobiles to encourage a shift to mass transit.

Finally, the issues of municipal finance are now almost everywhere in the country the same. In every city, there is enormous increase in municipal costs, tremendous pressure on tax resources, a desperate search for new taxes, and increasing insistence that state and federal governments take over the costs of large branches of municipal services. Welfare is the leading candidate. In some cases, states pay all or most of the burden (in New York, there is still a very large city share). And the federal government, in the Family Assistance Plan reform, begins to accept the responsibility of taking on a larger share, and perhaps ultimately the total cost. Even if this plan does not become law, any plan that succeeds it must move in the direction of the federal government paying a larger share or all of welfare costs. There are now demands that the federal government take on the costs of education.

The financial crisis of the cities is universal. What still perhaps remains distinctive about New York, and what the analysis of its budget indicates most clearly, is the enormous role of increases in costs of municipal labor as a factor in increasing the costs of city government. Here indeed is one area where some change is necessary if the cities are to become viable. Americans used to pride themselves on the fact that in this productive society it was not true that the best jobs were with government, as was true in developing countries where everyone scrambled to get on the government payroll. It is a wry commentary on recent developments that municipal jobs, in New York City at least, have become, in salary, in fringe benefits, and in seniority, better than jobs in the private sector.

So these studies are not only of New York—they are, by implication, studies of the American city. A second factor makes them important: their style of analysis. They are studies by economists. But as against so many of these, they are not academic studies. They demonstrate the remarkable advance that we saw in the sixties in the application of the tools of economic analysis to various problems, a development which has permitted us a much better insight into our urban problems. Admittedly not all our problems are to be illuminated by these techniques. Political scientists, sociologists, and historians, and even philosophers, have a good deal of light to shed on our present situation. Yet to my mind the economists have the most important light: they tell us which of the things we are doing simply don't seem to be worthwhile, to "pay." Political scientists, sociologists, and historians may give us reasons why we nevertheless keep on doing them, but at least the first step to improvement is to know whether they are worthwhile, not what interests they serve, or what role satisfaction they give, or how they got started.

Thus, when we learn, as we do in the education chapter, how much more we pay for the very modest improvement in achievement recorded by students in the More Effective Schools program, we have certainly learned something very useful. Perhaps we maintain this program as a means of employing more teachers or teacher aides as a means of responding to parental demands to do something, or because the teachers' union demands it. But let us at least know what it does for educational achievement. Similarly, it is useful to discover that it is easier to secure funds for capital investment on our subways than to acquire the amounts needed for adequate maintenance—millions for new equipment, relatively little for upkeep. Again there are reasons for this in the political realm. But the location of a problem of a misuse of resources in terms of efficiency is certainly by itself a contribution to our capacity to act. These essays are both sophisticated in their analysis and yet directly responsive to the urban issues they deal with. They are essays for citizens, rather than economists, but using all the tools of analysis that have been developed in recent years.

The style of analysis demonstrates a marked advantage over most discussions of urban problems, which characteristically take the form of the denunciation of one villain (the mayor, his party, the machine, the unions, the state government, the federal government, the property owners and taxpayers, the banks, the minorities, and so on), and the proposal of one solution (ban automobiles, community control of schools, public low-cost housing, federal tax sharing, and so on). There are many variants which these simpler approaches to urban problems take. Even the very knowledgeable John Kenneth Galbraith was recorded as saying a few years ago that New York City has no problems that another billion dollars will not solve, or words to that effect. In the few years since that statement was made, New York City has been able to find another three or four billion to spend every year, with no discernible impact on its problems. No one should dismiss the importance of money in dealing with urban problems; but even great sums of money may achieve nothing in the absence of a sound analysis and understanding.

When one reviews the range of programs and proposals that have been made—and in fact implemented—to improve the situation of cities since 1960, and considers the analyses in this volume, a third important theme emerging from these studies becomes apparent: there are no simple solutions anymore. There seems to be no one crux of the matter which, once grasped, gives us understanding and solution. The range of problems in our great cities is complex indeed and comes from many different sources: changes in demographic patterns, in the economy, in migration, in ethnic composition, in the scope and capacity of government, in mismatches between governmental responsibilities and resources, and many others. The catalog is endless. And the unfortunate conclusion of recent years is: it is hard to argue this or that part of it is unimportant. There is unfortunately no way of making the problem simple.

One element that is suggested by this complexity is that solutions are to be found in many quarters. Inevitably, government, at its various levels, must take the largest responsibility for solutions. Yet again and again in recent years we have seen important potential roles for business organization. Admittedly the more extravagant hopes that were placed on a business commitment to help solve the problems of cities have not been realized. Business investment in the ghettos has not stopped their decline. Investment in job training has not dried up the pool of those who cannot or will not work; investment in educational technology has not done much for educational problems.

But one can say pretty much the same about governmental programs, and it would be hard to say that one has been more successful than the other.

The notion of a business role in dealing with the problems of our cities—whether in pollution, education, poverty, housing, transportation, or strengthening of the general economic base of cities—is not a simple one. The business role emerges in many different ways. As our faith in single, simple solutions—even if of monumental scale—declines, since the experience of the sixties shows that such faith is poorly founded, inevitably we look more sympathetically on other sources of contributions to urban problems. These analyses suggest a place for the business role. They scarcely exhaust its possibilities. But in each of the areas of concern dealt with in these studies there is a persuasive case that the remarkable resources of American business enterprise, resources of knowledge, organization, capacities for implementation, can be put to better use in attacking urban problems.

This book appears at a time when American morale is low—low because of what are quite properly seen as foreign and domestic failures. It is my judgment that morale is probably presently lower than the best analysis would justify. There is another aspect to each of these problems, an aspect that might encourage us. Our environmental problems, severe as they are, also represent a remarkable success in making available automobiles and other energy-using devices to vast numbers of people and in opening up to people, more than any other nation has, the ability to realize individual desires for homes, transportation, recreation. This is not to gainsay the frightful environmental problems that have followed. But there must be a way of utilizing the resources of intelligence and organization that have produced the first in the service of the second. Our educational problems in part derive from our ambitions, which aim to bring many years of education to all people. Inevitably, this extension, which few other countries have attempted, brings a good number of problems in its wake. Our housing problems derive from our success in building so many better houses on the outskirts of our cities. Abandonment reflects terrible problems, but they are not so much problems of insufficiency of housing as problems of its upgrading—problems of better housing and neighborhood competing with worse housing and neighborhood. And our problems of public transportation derive from the fact that so many Americans have private transportation.

I do not mean to downgrade the urgency of the problems. I mean to suggest that perhaps our morale is lower than it should be, and that there are many approaches and many sources of power, those of private business as well as principally those of government, which it is now incumbent upon us to develop and implement. The analyses in this volume, produced as they were by a private financial organization as a public service, are a contribution to that end.

Nathan Glazer, sociologist, educator, and author, first achieved national prominence in 1950 as coauthor with David Riesman and Reuel Denney of *The Lonely Crowd; A study of the Changing American Character,* a book described as among the most influential works of descriptive sociology published in the United States in the twentieth century. Later with Daniel Patrick Moynihan, he wrote *Beyond the Melting Pot,* an award-winning study on race and ethnic relations in New York City. Holder of a doctorate from Columbia University, Glazer has traveled widely, studying and lecturing. During the early sixties, he interrupted his academic career to serve as urban sociologist with the Housing and Home Finance Agency in Washington, D.C., helping inaugurate domestic projects that became the nucleus of the government's anti-poverty programs. Since 1969 he has been Professor of Education and Social Structure at Harvard University.

Metropolis

The central cities have played a most significant role in the evolution of this country. As the United States became established as a major industrial nation, its cities grew in areas favored by river and ocean inlet locations. They frequently served as gateways for the movement of goods and people between the old world and the new, and developed as business centers for the surrounding regions.

While the cities' matchless agglomeration and diversities constitute some of their greatest assets, they also pose unique problems. The apparent incompatability between size and concentration of activity in core cities on the one hand, and easy accessibility to uncrowded amenities on the other, has created environmental and adaptive difficulties. Satisfying the need for proper housing, jobs, transportation, recreation, and other facilities for their millions of residents would be no mean task under any circumstances.

Especially in recent decades, migrants from rural areas have joined those from abroad in the metropolitan population centers, a movement which challenges local governments throughout the country. In this age of concern over population growth, the rural sections of the nation are being depopulated, and as their towns try to survive, metropolitan centers must cope with expanding populations.

THE CITIES AND THEIR REGIONS Although the population is becoming more concentrated in metropolitan areas, it is the suburbs rather than the core cities which are growing most rapidly. As a result, an increasing number of persons are moving to less densely settled neighborhoods even as the urban population increases. Metropolitan areas as a whole gained 17 percent in population in the decade of the 1960s, while their central cities grew by but 6 percent. In the same period, many smaller and older cities declined in population. St. Louis lost 19 percent, and Cleveland and Pittsburgh each lost about 15 percent, for example. However, the number of people in New York City rose somewhat, and cities such as Phoenix and Houston gained nearly one-third.

Increasingly, the newer sections of the metropolitan areas have developed outside of the central cities, whose boundaries have not expanded along with the growth of their regions. Automobile ownership and new roads have made it easier to drive to office, shopping, and entertainment activities without entering the population core. Development and growth of the new suburbs and exurbs have left the central cities increasingly to the poorer segments of the population, who must inhabit the older neighborhoods and structures. The shift in the composition of the cities' population also presents many challenges. Central cities look in envy at the growing communities around them and in fright at the outmigration of the middle class.

The Negro population of New York City increased from 92,000, or 2 percent of the population, in 1910 to 1.7 million, or 22 percent, in 1970. Another group whose numbers have grown in New York City are persons of Puerto Rican extraction, estimated at nearly 900,000 in 1970. But New York City's share of racial minorities is small compared with the proportion in other major cities; blacks account for over two-thirds of the population of the District of Columbia and for over half of the populations of Newark and Atlanta.

The cities have always led newcomers into broader participation in American life, and the recent growth of their minority concentrations is the modern manifestation of that role. The latest newcomers suffer the intertwined problems of low income and adjustment to urban living. Both have contributed to the large proportion of persons who are on welfare in many central cities, which has reached over 10 percent in places such as Boston, Baltimore, Newark, and New York.

The central cities face the sometimes conflicting problems of responding to the needs of their low-income populations while at the same time trying to attract once again the middle- and high-income groups who can provide the resources and leadership needed to assure the cities' vitality. An enlarged population of economically and socially handicapped persons has created great strains on those cities trying to sustain the costly services mandated by rising social standards. Nevertheless, many have sustained their crucial role in providing places where the underprivileged can achieve economic progress.

Many jobs have moved in conjunction with the movement in population. In the New York region, the number of jobs in the suburbs rose by 35 percent in the sixties, while the city gained but 6 percent. The counties on the periphery of the region showed the largest proportional gains. Yet these suburban jobs are widely spaced in the broad area surrounding the city. New York City continues to be the hub of the regional economy, containing over half of its employment. It remains, and in the foreseeable future will continue to remain, the regional location with the greatest concentration by far of economic activity and employment opportunities.

DYNAMIC SERVICE AND OFFICE SECTORS

Because a broad range of goods and services is produced in, and distributed nationally from, metropolitan regions such as New York, their economic growth is closely related to that of the nation. New York's long-term economic health largely depends on the share of growing industries which it holds, and on the area's ability to attract such industries in competition with other locales.

The region's employment distribution shows strength in the service, government, and finance sectors, all of which are relatively insensitive to recession cutbacks. Its strong service orientation cushions it from the strongest effects of business cycles as well as from changing conditions in individual industries. Durable-goods manufacturing, cyclically more sensitive, accounts for a significantly smaller share in this region than in the nation as a whole. Similarly, employment in New York City's central administrative offices is more stable than are jobs on the assembly line.

Other cities and their surrounding regions are less fortunate. Seattle, for example, is heavily dependent on defense contracts, and shifts in federal government spending can, and have, created serious dislocations there. Detroit is heavily dependent on automobile production, an industry in which growth in employment has been sluggish and which is subject to significant shocks from changing short-term economic conditions. In mid-1970, the Department of Labor reported the rate of unemployment in Seattle and Detroit to have been 10.4 percent and 8.8 percent, respectively. By contrast, the New York labor market was reported to have an unemployment rate of only 4.4 percent at the same time.

Even mature economies in many older metropolitan regions have demonstrated a vigorous dynamism in their tradeoff between the broadly defined goods-producing sectors and the service industries. The industrial mix in many metropolitan regions, such as New York, is geared to the fast-growing finance, services, and government sectors. These sectors have absorbed ever greater proportions of the work force as part of redeployment toward a service-oriented, postindustrial economy. The change includes continuous progress in communications and implementation of computer-aided systems and management evaluation and control techniques.

On the other hand, goods production has diminished in relative importance as a source of employment in many metropolitan regions and in the nation as a whole. In slow-growing regions, an absolute, as well as relative, loss of jobs in the manufacturing sector has resulted.

These developments have enhanced the importance of the metropolitan areas, where one can find the concentration of people and talent capable of pursuing the new tasks. The central cities are not alone in the expansion of communications-oriented white-collar activities. But the cities are unique in the scale and diversities of such activities undertaken within their boundaries.

A significant indication of the economic leadership role of the cities is their sustained preeminence as locales for central office activities. New York is often used as an example of a city losing its central office function. Yet, during the 1960s, 90 million square feet of office space was constructed in Manhattan alone, almost half as much as existed there in the early 1960s. According to *Fortune's* latest lists, 126 of the 500 largest industrial corporations in the United States are headquartered in the New York region, as well as 4 of the top 10 utilities, 5 of the 7 largest banks, 3 of the top 4 largest insurance companies, and many major airlines and retailers.

The recent departure of several major corporate headquarters from New York has also caused much concern. But in the same period, other large firms have moved into the city and many have expanded within it. Of the largest 250 industrial corporations in the United States, 83 had their head offices in New York City in 1970, an increase of 10 during the previous decade. Among the second largest 250 firms, there has been a significant decline in the number headquartered in the city—from 58 in 1960 and 53 in 1967 to only 35 in 1970.

THE FISCAL CHALLENGE The "crisis" of the central cities is sometimes more a matter of rhetoric than fact, but many cities face most difficult hurdles. The problem for individual cities is related both to rate of growth and to geographic size. The newer and more rapidly growing population centers in the West, and increasingly in the new South, are doing better than many cities in the older northeastern and north central part of the country. Geographically small central cities such as Boston and Detroit face difficulties not experienced to the same extent by cities such as New York and Washington, D.C., which are large enough to contain improving neighborhoods even as others suffer deterioration.

With all their problems, central cities often have huge resources, with above-average per capita incomes, high property value, and vigorous economic activity. The giant budgets of many central cities are indicative, not only of high costs, but also of the increasing level of many public services and the high level of resources which can be tapped within them. In New York City, for example, local government outlays have increased over the years in part because of substantial increases in school personnel, greater opportunities for free higher education, and better opportunities for health care for lower-income families.

Yet despite the cities' huge resources and a willingness to allot increasingly large amounts of money toward alleviating human needs, the problem of poverty persists. It is a fact of life for millions; it lingers like an ineradicable disorder, refusing to yield to solutions couched wholly in terms of money. Progress in curbing poverty may be forever beyond our reach until there is broader understanding of its psychology as well as its economic basis. A bishop, now retired, understood this. Gazing up at the unfinished spires of a cathedral on Manhattan's West Side, he said it would be finished when the poorest asked why it was not finished.

Poverty and Economic Development in New York City

THE PEOPLE
AND THE ECONOMY Never before in history has a community attempted to eradicate poverty. It has been man's assumption that poverty, like the mountains and the seas, is always with us. While there are records of efforts to help the forlorn and helpless, until recently the outer limits of such help took the form of orphanages, the poorhouse, and the old folks' home. Not until modern times has man seriously begun to consider the broad problem of poverty with the ultimate hope of erasing it from the land. Out of these considerations have come programs that already consume half a community's revenue. These efforts have produced results. They have eased hardships and promised hope. And in doing so, the war on poverty has generated results that could not be anticipated. It has produced an impatience and discontentment with conditions the poor once accepted as immutable.

Poverty can be examined from different angles, but fundamentally it is an economic malady. There is a cause-and-effect relationship between poverty and the many cultural, psychological, and sociological problems that fester, and the view here is that the most productive course is to consider first the role of economic development in alleviating these problems. It is within this framework that business and the economic elements of the community can make their most constructive contribution.

The economy of New York City is huge, healthy, stable, and growing. It is also fragmented, small-scale, volatile, and vulnerable. The city's people are industrious, entrepreneurial, productive, and prosperous. Also, many are poverty-stricken, unaware of or uninterested in opportunities, inefficient, and unable to participate effectively. Much of the city's physical structure is brand new, exploiting fully the latest innovations in production, communication, and management controls. But there remain many old, dilapidated, obsolete establishments. The city stands in the forefront of the new service- and computer-oriented economy. Yet, it embraces many thousands of small, marginal, and outmoded businesses. It stands as a beacon of the better life to come, but the promise is dulled by residual decay. Change and stagnation, shimmering new buildings and wretched slums, vigor and decadence, confidence and despair, all exist in the same place and at the same time.

How does one describe this statistically? Altogether about 8 million persons reside within New York's geographical confines. Its economy provides approximately 4.1 million jobs serving a complete range of industrial activities.

The city's residents comprised 4 percent of the national population in 1970, and earned about 5 percent of its personal income. Thus New Yorkers' per capita receipts are 25 percent higher than the national average. Nevertheless, nonresidents holding jobs here have tended to acquire an increasing proportion of all wages and salaries paid out in the city. And while New York has enjoyed sustained real growth in total and average income, the continued influx of poverty-stricken nonwhites and Puerto Ricans has helped prevent any discernible improvement in the family-income structure of the major ghetto areas.

DEMOGRAPHIC PATTERNS   On the surface, indicators show relatively small aggregate changes during the sixties in New York City's population and employment. Behind the facade, however, significant shifts have occurred in the racial and age characteristics of the population, in its occupational composition, and in the industrial deployment of the work force.

As a consequence of the continued net outmigration of whites, accompanied by sustained immigration of blacks and Puerto Ricans,

by 1970 the proportion of whites had diminished to about 65 percent of the city's population, and the nonwhites and Puerto Ricans constituted about 23 and 12 percent, respectively.

In comparison with the white population, the nonwhite and Puerto Rican groups are quite young and have become more youthful over time. As indicated in the table, since 1960 white children under the age of 15 have held steady as a proportion of the white population, while the under-15 age groups of the nonwhites and Puerto Ricans have grown markedly in relative importance. About a third of the white population is under the age of 25, but almost half of the non-whites and three-fifths of the Puerto Ricans are in this category.

The Changing Age Composition of New York City's Ethnic Groups (percentage distribution by group)

	White		Nonwhite		Puerto Rican	
	1960	1970	1960	1970	1960	1966
65 and over	12.4	14.0	4.8	5.3	2.0	2.8
25 to 64	54.7	49.4	51.6	45.4	41.8	37.1
15 to 24	11.7	15.5	13.1	17.1	18.8	17.8
Under 15	21.2	21.1	30.5	32.2	37.4	42.3

SOURCE: U.S. Bureau of the Census and the Population Health Survey.

The age composition of nonwhites and Puerto Ricans exerts a strong effect on the labor market, and the impact will become even greater in the near future. Workers under the age of 25 traditionally have had great difficulty in finding stable employment. In 1970, almost 26 percent of all Negro teen-agers were unemployed. Even higher unemployment rates prevailed in the ghetto areas of the city, where on the average 28 percent of black teen-agers and about 34 percent of Puerto Ricans sought jobs unsuccessfully.

OCCUPATION-JOB MISMATCH Although the total number of jobs in New York City grew only moderately during the sixties, their occupational composition shifted markedly in response to changing industrial needs. The most important growth occurred in the professional group. On the other end of the scale, and not surprisingly, the greatest occupational losses occurred among the operatives and laborers groups.

The changing pattern of industrial employment in New York City reflects growth in those industries whose occupational composition is predominantly white-collar. Conversely, those industries registering the largest job losses tend to employ a much higher proportion of blue-collar workers. These trends have caused apprehension concerning the capacity of the local economy to provide a sufficient number of reasonably remunerative jobs to the occupationally handicapped.

Recent events, however, indicate a somewhat greater compatibility between jobs and people than was previously expected. For example, nonwhites have made rapid strides in increasing their representation among the white-collar occupations. In 1960, 29 percent of the nonwhite labor force was employed in white-collar jobs; by 1970, the proportion had risen to 42 percent. This was a much bigger gain than that of the white labor force, where 55 percent were employed in white-collar jobs in 1960 and 63 percent by 1970.

Occupational Distribution of Employment in New York City

	1970		1960	
	White, %	Nonwhite, %	White, %	Nonwhite, %
Total	100	100	100	100
White-collar	63	42	55	29
Professional	16	11	13	7
Managerial	12	4	10	3
Clerical and sales work	35	27	32	19
Blue-collar	27	34	34	41
Service	10	25	10	30

SOURCE: U.S. Bureau of Labor Statistics.
NOTE: Totals may not agree because of rounding.

Encouraging as these statistics may be, it is reasonable to question whether or not progress is occurring at a sufficiently rapid rate. Despite some growth in the minority proportion of professional and technical workers, hardly any advance took place in their representation in the managers and proprietors category. Most of the gain occurred in the clerical-worker group of the white-collar sector, which tends to be lower paid and predominantly female.

The problem of matching skills to job openings shows up most dramatically when the occupational structure of ghetto unemployed is compared with anticipated city job openings. Here the seriousness of the experience-opportunity mismatch—the skills gap—becomes particularly apparent.

Approximately three-fourths of all New York City job openings (estimated at 1,250,000 between 1965 and 1975) will be in the white-collar and craftsmen categories, while only 16 percent of the slum-area jobless in 1966 had previous experience in such occupations. At the other end of the spectrum, over half the unemployed were formerly employed as laborers (or had never worked at all), while less than

The Skills Gap

	Occupation Distribution of Ghetto Unemployed, 1966, %	Estimated Job Openings,* 1965–1975, %
White-collar	13.6	65.7
Craftsmen	2.8	7.4
Operatives	14.7	7.7
Service	16.6	18.6
Laborers and others	52.3	0.6

*Resulting from industrial change, deaths, and retirements.
SOURCE: U.S. Bureau of Labor Statistics and New York State Department of Labor, Division of Research and Statistics.

1 percent of the employment opportunities will fall in this classification.

Despite these gloomy data, it is possible to conclude this discussion on a somewhat encouraging note. A close examination of job growth patterns in the New York area makes it apparent that opportunities will grow "most rapidly for those persons with the highest levels of educational attainment, but in terms of total labor demand, the vast number of jobs to be filled will require something less than a college degree."[1] As many as three-fourths of the job openings in the next five years will go to workers with a high school education or less.

PROBLEMS, GOALS, AND NEEDS Review of the New York City economic situation reveals a reasonably healthy, stable economy, in advanced stages of postindustrial development. The changing ethnic population mix, however, and the shifting industrial base have helped create mutually reinforcing problems. These are revealed by the poverty concentrations, the dreary slums and the attendant unemployment, underemployment, and associated socioeconomic ills. They underscore the necessity of increasing the per capita income of ghetto residents and their level of employment, as well as their potential for higher wage employment through enhanced personal productivity.

The root of the trouble, as indicated earlier, lies in the skills gap of so many of the city's residents. Measures to overcome this disparity must be implemented. It is estimated that in 1970 about 30 percent of the jobs in the city paid wages of less than $90 a week. Effective job training could increase the personal income of currently unskilled or underskilled workers by making it possible for them to escape from low-wage employment and move up career ladders.

[1] Herbert Bienstock, "Manpower Directions in New York City in the 70's," *City Almanac*, December 1970.

In view of the current high school dropout rate and generally low level of educational attainment, it remains urgent to provide an adequate number of low-skill entry-level jobs for disadvantaged city residents. Pursuing this goal may require arresting the exodus of industrial firms from the city. We know that a major reason for this outmigration is lack of space. In the past, policy makers have exercised a strong bias in favor of using the city's land resources for residential rather than industrial purposes. More recently, however, the city has adopted a more balanced land-use policy.

At the same time, it must be kept in mind that the service-producing sectors of this city's economy promise most in providing jobs and income. Job training and occupational expectations should be so oriented. Implications of this continuing shift to services include growing job opportunities for women and older workers, increased opportunities for self-employment, growing importance of small, specialized firms, and greater need for workers with more formal education.

The per capita output of slum dwellers may be low, but that of New York City is not. The city's future growth depends on improving the psychological, social, and technical preparation of its labor force. With adequate, qualified manpower, New York may continue to exploit its "external economies"—the proliferation of business and advantages which have afforded this city an environment of leadership in the developing postindustrial, service-oriented economy.

POVERTY AND THE GHETTOS

CONCEPTS AND SCOPE

Although strong economic growth such as this nation has been experiencing for the past decade has diminished poverty, it has not eliminated it. Poverty persists, and remains particularly evident in urban areas such as New York City. Too often, however, discussions of how to cope with poverty generate more heat than light, since concepts are fuzzy, fact and fiction are mixed indiscriminately, and some population groups have become so identified in the public's mind with poverty that the problem is often viewed as a racial one, with its economic aspects overlooked.

What is poverty? Simply stated, a household living in poverty is one whose total income is insufficient to support minimum living standards. As applied to 1969 incomes, for example, poverty in nonfarm areas, as defined by the Social Security Administration, ranges from $1,751 for a woman 65 or older living alone, through $3,743 for a four-member family, to $6,101 for a family of seven or more

persons. These are national estimates. For the New York City area, where living costs are relatively high, an even larger income must be maintained to escape poverty as officially defined.

The number of people in New York City who live in poverty is one of those indeterminate quantities that haunt and frustrate policy makers. Every ten years the Bureau of the Census collects comprehensive family-income facts which provide the basis for much social and economic analysis. Exact enumeration of the poor is difficult, however, as they are often missed entirely or incorrectly counted when the census enumerators make their rounds. Further problems develop because of the absence of comparable data relating family income to family size in noncensus years.

Trends in personal income mirror well the impact of economic progress generally, but provide limited insight on the way that growth is distributed among the population. Per capita personal income in New York City grew by about 24 percent between 1959 and 1969, in constant dollar terms. If the incomes of each family reported in the census had been increased by such a percentage, the proportion of impoverished families would have fallen markedly during the ten-year period. Using a $4,000 family income (constant 1969 dollars) as a rough approximation of the poverty floor, about 16 percent of the approximately 2.0 million families in the city were impoverished in 1969—the same proportion as in 1959.[1]

The ratio of white families living in poverty was practically identical in 1959 and 1969, while the ratio of nonwhite families living in poverty dropped by approximately 9 percentage points. This increased income level for nonwhites in the city reflects better job and training opportunities during the peak employment years of 1968 and 1969, higher wages, and more families receiving public assistance with higher average benefit levels.

POVERTY AND RACE Despite their imperfections, average income statistics do reflect the relative growth of income among minority groups in New York City. Median income of nonwhite families (which was about $4,400 at the time of the 1960 census) stood at almost $6,900 in 1969. This would indicate, after taking cost-of-living increases into account, an increase in real income of almost 20 percent. This growth was slightly more than the 15 percent rate enjoyed by white families. Poverty occurred

---

[1]Blanche Bernstein, *Welfare and Income in New York City*, Center for New York City Affairs, New School for Social Research, August 1971.

NEW YORK CITY FAMILIES BY ETHNIC GROUPS

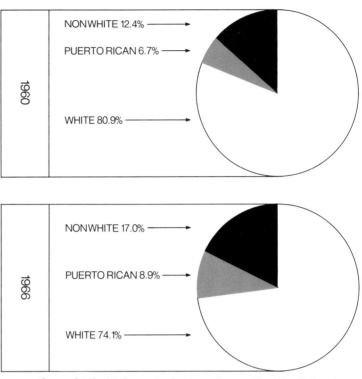

1960

NONWHITE 12.4% ———→

PUERTO RICAN 6.7% ———→

WHITE 80.9% ———————→

1966

NONWHITE 17.0% ———→

PUERTO RICAN 8.9% ———→

WHITE 74.1% ———————→

SOURCE: Center for Social Research, Graduate Center, The City University of New York.

among 19 percent of nonwhite families in 1969 as compared to 15 percent of white families.

Even the nonwhites, however, are better off than another ethnic group, the Puerto Ricans. The median income of Puerto Rican families in New York City in 1959 was about $3,800, and over 33 percent of them were in the under-$3,000 category. An earlier study by Dr. Bernstein[1] shows that median income of this growing segment of the city's population in 1968 was about $5,100, a real increase of 9 percent over the 1959 level. Puerto Rican median family income has thus grown less rapidly than that of nonwhites (11 percent between 1959 and 1968), and its absolute level in 1968 was about $800 less (87 percent) of that category.

With all the emphasis on minority groups, it should not be forgotten that the absolute number of white families (other than Puerto Ricans) with low incomes is also substantial. In 1959, almost 200,000 (63

[1]Blanche Bernstein, "The Distribution of Income in New York City," *The Public Interest,* Summer 1970.

percent) of the 317,000 families with incomes under $3,000 were white. Of course, the great majority of families in the city in 1960 were white (88 percent). By 1969, the share was somewhat smaller. Nevertheless, it appears that over two-fifths of the impoverished families in the city today are white, while roughly one-third are black and perhaps about one-fourth are Puerto Ricans.

PERCENT OF NEW YORK CITY FAMILIES WITH FOUR OR MORE PERSONS, BY ETHNIC GROUPS

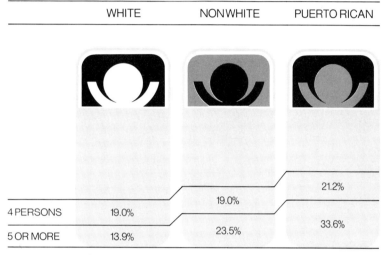

	WHITE	NONWHITE	PUERTO RICAN
4 PERSONS	19.0%	19.0%	21.2%
5 OR MORE	13.9%	23.5%	33.6%

SOURCE: Adapted from New York City Department of Health, Population Characteristics, 1964.

This comparison becomes more dramatic when we consider the fact that families of minority groups—particularly Puerto Ricans—tend to be considerably larger than white families, as shown in the chart. This is not an isolated phenomenon. The fertility (childbearing) rate among the poor throughout the nation is 56 percent greater than among the rest of the population. To put it in simple terms, one of the main reasons why there are so many poor people is that the poor produce such large families.

All things considered, it appears as if about one or more out of every six families and one or more out of every five people in New York City are living in poverty.

THE OUTLOOK FOR POVERTY IN THE CITY

The persistence of poverty in the face of general income growth makes it evident that, unless special measures are taken to extricate the poor from that status, their number in the future—as in the sixties—may not show any perceptible decline. Certainly the concentration of poverty among minority groups in the city will, in the absence of any policy measures to the contrary, become even more pronounced. To a large extent, this will result from migration patterns which will probably see the continuation of an influx of poor blacks and Puerto Ricans, with whites and some of the better-off blacks leaving for the suburbs.

No one knows for sure, but the relatively new "two-way" Negro migration may be a modern manifestation of New York's traditional "crucible" or "incubator" role whereby the more successful of the immigrant (or, more recently in-migrant) groups move out to the suburbs while their place is taken by newer waves of the poor coming into the city.

Even if there were no net immigration of minority groups into the city, their numbers here would increase because they are younger and have higher rates of natural increase (births minus deaths) than do the whites. Their poverty, moreover, is more concentrated among the young, while the poverty of white families (other than Puerto Ricans) is relatively more prevalent among the older groups. It appears, for instance, that about one-half of the whites but less than one-fifth of the blacks and under one-tenth of the Puerto Ricans who receive public assistance in the city are aged 50 or over.

POVERTY AND UNEMPLOYMENT In comparison to whites, minority groups do not fare too well in the job market. According to a study by the Bureau of Labor Statistics, the 1970 nonwhite unemployment rate in New York City stood at 5.4 percent,[1] in contrast to 4.7 percent for whites. Since the white figure, moreover, is raised by the inclusion of Puerto Ricans, the true gap between the whites exclusive of Puerto Ricans and the minority groups is even wider.

There is, of course, a clear connection between poverty and unemployment. Obviously, the impact of poverty is most severe on those groups that are at a competitive disadvantage in the labor market. The main determinant of a family's economic well-being continues to be the earning power of the family head.

The twin—and interrelated—problems of poverty and unemployment are particularly acute in the large ghetto areas of New York City.[2] A review of the low-income areas of the city demonstrates the

[1] Even this high rate was, however, lower than nonwhite unemployment rates in all the other ten central cities surveyed, except Washington, D.C. and Chicago. The rate in Baltimore was the same as in New York.

[2] This is not uniquely a New York City phenomenon. As pointed out recently in the *Business Review* of the Federal Reserve Bank of Philadelphia, "Increasingly, the urban ghettos in the central cities of large metropolitan areas continue to be repositories for those on the low end of the economic totem pole."

fact that major poverty areas tend to coincide with or incorporate the largely black ghettos of Central Harlem and Bedford-Stuyvesant, the Puerto Rican enclave of East Harlem, the heavily Puerto Rican and black South Bronx, and Manhattan's historic lower East Side, where newer immigrants (primarily Puerto Ricans) are taking the places of older poor immigrant groups.

Family income in the ghetto areas of New York City was substantially below the overall average city family income in 1960. This disparity persisted during the sixties. According to a Bureau of Labor Statistics survey, the 1968–69 median family income in the city's poverty areas was $5,500, as compared to $8,289 for all New York City families. In real dollars, this represented an apparent 10 percent gain for residents of the poverty areas over the 1959 level. Despite this improvement, the relationship between income levels of ghetto residents and the rest of the city has remained almost constant, with median income of families in poverty neighborhoods hovering around two-thirds of the level attained by all New York City families.

One reason for this apparent stagnation in the relative income status of ghetto residents during the sixties may be that it is not precisely the same group of people who are being measured in both cases. Two significant changes have been taking place which have a bearing on this point. In the first place, the populations of the ghetto areas have been falling.

Area Population	1970	1960	% Change, 1960–1970
Central Harlem	161,065	213,783	− 24.7
East Harlem	141,239	163,677	− 13.7
Bedford-Stuyvesant	218,887	225,425	− 2.9
South Bronx	138,934	154,700	− 10.2

SOURCE: 1960 and 1970 censuses of population.

At the same time, it appears that the share of blacks and Puerto Ricans in the ghettos, already high in 1960, climbed to even higher levels by 1969. For instance, while the total Bedford-Stuyvesant population fell by 3 percent in the past decade, the nonwhite population in the area increased, from 161,000 to 179,000 for a gain of 11 percent. It would appear that more nonwhites were entering than leaving the area, and there are very few white holdouts. The nonwhite population of Bedford-Stuyvesant in 1970 was 83 percent of the total, compared with 72 percent in 1960. Thus, residents who were better off, particularly whites, left the ghettos, to be replaced by new entrants with incomes probably well below the ghetto medians. Median family income of blacks in the South stood at $4,278 in 1968, or 28 percent below the level for their counterparts in New York City's poverty areas.

Needless to say, unemployment rates in the ghetto areas are substantially above average. The very high Puerto Rican ghetto unemployment rate is consistent with that group's bottom position on both the city's and the nation's income scales.

New York City Poverty Area Unemployment Rates	1968–69, %	1969–70, %
Total	6.8	7.9
White	4.5	7.1
Negro	6.4	7.3
Puerto Rican	9.5	9.5

SOURCE: U.S. Bureau of Labor Statistics.

However bleak, these data actually understate the seriousness of the unemployment problems in the ghettos. Conventional measurements take no account of the special problems of limited employment, low-wage employment, or the omission from the unemployment count of those who have despaired of ever finding a job and have quit the labor force. There is also an understatement resulting from the non-count of males who are known to be present in the community but who do not show up in the population statistics. The Bureau of Labor Statistics estimated that in 1968–1969 two-fifths of the almost 400,000 working-age persons living in New York City's poverty areas were neither employed nor seeking employment; still others were under-employed—that is, working full-time but earning less than $65 per week.

This cursory survey of the extent of poverty and unemployment in major ghetto areas leads to the conclusion that, just as New York City is a crucible for the nation's poor, so the large black and Puerto Rican ghettos, while not containing the majority of the city's poor, nevertheless seem to have become the crucibles of poverty within the city. To the extent that society wishes to eliminate poverty, it must obviously make a broad-based attack on these problems, with appropriate attention being paid to the ghettos where the concentration of poverty is most acute, and seemingly most intractable.

Any review of the phenomenon of poverty in New York City, particularly its prevalence among blacks and Puerto Ricans, is at once foreboding, challenging, and promising. It is foreboding because the city's economy and social structure cannot long endure so large a share of its population suffering from the chronic slum ills of bad housing, poor education, inadequate job training, high unemployment, family instability, and very low incomes.

The challenge lies in the obligation to implement the promise of equal opportunity via an improved educational system and more effective job recruitment and training. The opportunity exists to prepare economically handicapped blacks and Puerto Ricans for more productive participation as workers, and more constructive involvement as citizens, by cutting off their destructive inheritance of joblessness and welfare as an expected way of life.

WELFARE AND ALL THAT

THE "SYSTEM"

An elaborate public welfare system constitutes our response to poverty. Generally, people are eligible for welfare if their income is less than they must have to meet their regular and special needs and they are either aged, blind, disabled, dependent children, or the parents of dependent children when the breadwinner is either deceased, absent, disabled, or unable to find an adequate job.

Public assistance in New York City, as elsewhere in the nation, consists of six programs dealing with the separate categories of need:

1. Old Age Assistance (OAA).
2. Aid to the Disabled (AD).
3. Assistance to the Blind (AB).
4. Aid to Dependent Children (ADC).
5. Aid to Dependent Children—Unemployed Parent (ADCU).
6. Home Relief (HR), including veterans' assistance.

The first five receive federal support. OAA, AD, and AB serve individuals while ADC and ADCU are family programs. The sixth, Home Relief, applies to families and individuals not eligible for any of the federally aided programs. It is used to supplement the incomes of families in which low earnings of the family head do not provide adequate support.

Currently, most categories of welfare allotments average about $80 per person per month, depending on the number of children, age composition of the family, and income. The payments begin after proof of need has been established and last as long as the need continues, with periodic reverification.

Generally, an individual's welfare grants are reduced by the amount of any outside income, with certain exceptions. In New York City, selected welfare recipients may receive some outside income without equivalent deductions from their welfare grants. In theory, all able-bodied adults receiving assistance, with the exception of those taking care of a dependent child, are required to look for work. Persons on either Home Relief or ADCU and over the age of 16 must register with the Division of Employment Rehabilitation.

WELFARE'S RISING ROLLS The number of welfare recipients in New York City is about 1.2 million, or 15 percent of the city's total population—quadruple the figure for 1960. Some authorities claim that continued increases on welfare rolls can be anticipated, moreover, because there is reason to believe that many people who are legally entitled to welfare payments may not have exploited this opportunity. Welfare rolls have increased markedly in some of the city's lower-middle-income areas. The rise in the number of white applicants may be due to changing attitudes about accepting welfare and is consistent with the significantly higher unemployment rate for white residents in poverty areas than in previous years.

Welfare Recipients in New York City, 1960–1971

Year, (December Data)	Number, (in thousands)	Annual Percentage Increase
1960	328	3
1961	352	7
1962	365	4
1963	415	14
1964	472	14
1965	531	13
1966	616	16
1967	787	28
1968	978	24
1969	1040	6
1970	1166	12
1971	1275	9

At the beginning of the decade the welfare rolls rose quite slowly, but accelerated in 1963, with the rate of growth peaking out in 1967. While the overall rise in 1970 did not equal the 1967 or 1968 increases, the recession in the last six months of that year saw 90,000 people added to the rolls.

Family-oriented programs absorb the lion's share of public welfare. This emphasis has become considerably more pronounced over time as these programs have skyrocketed, while recipients of aid to the aged, the disabled, and the blind have accounted for a constantly diminishing share of the welfare population. For example, clients in the Aid to Dependent Children programs reached 864,000 at the end of 1970, a level almost four times that of 1960. Home Relief recipients rose from 59,000 to 155,000 in that interim. On the other hand, despite the inclusion of drug addicts in the Aid to the Disabled program, the combined growth in that and the Old Age Assistance and Assistance to the Blind Programs grew only by a relatively modest 63,000, or 80 percent.

Locally, several interrelated factors have helped bring about the particularly large increases in income support payments. One is the growth in average payment per recipient. In New York City, the 1970 average grant level was half again as high as the level a decade earlier. As the level of welfare payments has risen, more of the population, especially those with fixed incomes, are eligible for relief, thus leading to an increase in number of recipients.

Another reason for the growth in caseload is the age distribution of the population: those persons in a dependent situation—children and the elderly—have increased relative to the total population. The Department of Social Services estimated that there were approximately 25,000 children born in New York City during 1970 to families receiving assistance, about 17 percent of total births in the city. A large portion of these births are to nonwhite and Puerto Rican mothers in the ADC program. The growth in the older white population, moreover, further contributes to the expansion of the welfare program.

Certain institutional changes, such as simplified declaration of need and higher acceptance rates by caseworkers, have made it easier for impoverished people to go on relief. Another factor which has affected the growth in the number of welfare recipients is the increased claims of poor people of their "right" to welfare. Part of the change in attitude has resulted from the civil rights movement. Much of it has occurred from the publicity that has been given to antipoverty programs as well as to the Medicaid program.

THE MATTER OF LARGE FAMILIES The rapidly increasing number of children swelling the welfare rolls provides the all too lamentable evidence that, in New York City at least, the rich get richer and the poor have children. The very fact of large families among the poor tends to perpetuate poverty. The more children there are in the family, the less the mother is able to work to supplement the family income, even if she had the incentive or ability to do so.

Americans generally recognize the population explosion as being associated with poverty, disease, and ignorance in other countries but do not apply this same reasoning to these phenomena in our own disadvantaged areas. In the United States, nonwhites and Puerto Ricans, the groups most affected by poverty, have higher fertility rates than whites. It is hoped that more widely available birth control information and the liberalization of New York's abortion laws will make it easier for women to choose how many children they will have. It is still too early to tell if abortion reform or family planning has caused a permanent or just a temporary reduction in fertility rates in New York City.

WELFARE'S RISING COSTS The rapid growth in the number of welfare recipients has meant substantial increases in the cost of welfare programs. The city's Human Resources Administration, which is responsible for administering the public welfare program, spent about $2 billion in fiscal 1971, a jump of almost 13 percent over the previous year and more than double the level of 1967–68.

Budget of Human Resource Administration (in millions of dollars)

	1970–71	1969–70	1968–69	1967–68
Income support	$1,602	$1,436	$1,003	$ 696
Individual and family services	267	229	174	155
Other	264	223	182	160
Total	$2,113	$1,888	$1,359	$1,011

SOURCE: The City of New York Executive Budget for appropriate years.

The bulk of the fiscal 1971 funds consisted of $1.6 billion in cash payments to welfare recipients and $300 million each in related services and administrative costs. The city contributes close to a third of this total and receives federal and state reimbursement for the remainder.

Funds for "individual and family services" cover the costs of providing counseling and supportive services to delinquent youth, dependent and neglected children, multiproblem poverty-area families, and dependent adults. The remaining funds are for various welfare-related activities such as manpower, early childhood, community development, and narcotics programs.

The fiscal squeeze on the city's expense budget resulting from increased welfare costs has become especially severe as welfare competes with other city services for relatively scarce funds. Welfare costs absorb a constantly increasing share of the city's expense budget (22 percent in fiscal 1971 as compared to 12 percent in 1965). The rapid rise in welfare rolls and costs in New York City, moreover, has been paralleled in states throughout the country. Indeed, whereas welfare had earlier been characterized as primarily a phenomenon associated with industrial areas, it has more recently become prevalent everywhere in the country. In New York State, for example, recent data show that the rate of increase in welfare rolls in the large upstate cities, suburbs, and rural areas was more than twice that of New York City.

Nationally, welfare rolls have risen by about 70 percent in the last five years and 7 percent in the first six months of 1971. As in New York, ADC has accounted for most of this increase. Over 14 million people were receiving public assistance in the United States at midyear 1971; over 10 million of them were on ADC. The federal share of welfare costs in 1970 reached $7.5 billion (including medical assistance and administrative costs), or about 52 percent of the total bill. In the face of welfare's rising fiscal and social costs almost everywhere in the country, the federal government has sought widespread welfare reform. President Nixon introduced a family-assistance plan to Congress in 1970, which included provisions for guaranteed family income of $2,400 for a family of four; expanded work incentives to encourage families to move from welfare to workfare; funding for more job training programs and day-care facilities; and the consolidation of the old age, blind, and disabled programs. The Administration's proposals offer a distinctly improved approach to the problem of welfare and poverty than the present hodgepodge of programs. Yet, in view of the many complex and diverse reasons for poverty in an increasingly affluent society, some questions can be raised as to the efficacy of any "solution" to this many-sided problem.

The accelerating growth of welfare would not be so surprising in an environment of economic decline and rising unemployment, such as that which prevailed in the thirties when the public welfare system was established. At that time, there was a large segment of the population for which there was no work.

New York City, in the second half of the sixties, strengthened its overall economic and employment situation. To be sure, the skill requirements in the city's changing economic structure are not conducive to enlarged job opportunities for the disadvantaged. However, the signal failure of the welfare approach is that it places almost all of its emphasis on the symptoms of the disease—poverty, unemployment, abandonment—and virtually none on the causes, which include the inability to earn adequate income due to the lack of appropriate job skills.

There are those who would argue that the employment question is not relevant, and cite the fact that almost four-fifths of welfare recipients are either dependent children or parents of such children. About 8 percent of the male recipients are categorized by the city as being "unemployed but employable," and an additional 3 percent are "underemployed." These men, however, may have the theoretical capability to support their families, thus removing 20 to 25 percent of all recipients from the welfare rolls if they could acquire well-paying jobs. These figures are not inconsistent with the finding that almost 30 percent of welfare mothers of dependent children have husbands living with them.

For the 40 percent of ADC women who have been separated or abandoned, the implications are not quite clear. The basic unknown is the extent to which fathers "desert" in order to enable the rest of the family to receive the full benefits of ADC grants accruing to the mothers and the now-dependent children, while the "errant" fathers are able to keep their wages without giving up welfare income. Obviously, the reasons for the high proportion of ADC mothers with absent husbands are more complex than mere income maximization, but the problem remains of finding incentives to encourage family stability. The fact remains that families with a low earning capacity which do stay together are penalized in the sense that they cannot achieve the same total income as divided families.

These aberrations result from the requirement that all or, under some recent innovations, most of earned income is subtracted from welfare payments, so that welfare substantially serves as an alternative to work. As such, it can, and does, function as a disincentive to assuming low-wage employment. It is indeed noteworthy that the recent rapid acceleration in the number of welfare recipients dates back to mid-1966, at which time the equivalent annual welfare incomes were revised upward, and, for a family of four, climbed well above the minimum wage income.

Since 1967, the welfare program has provided work incentives for most families on ADC. The first $30 of monthly earnings plus one-

third of the balance, plus an allowance for work expenses, can be retained with no reduction in welfare grants. The cutoff point is about $6,400. As of mid-1971, there were only 9,600 slots available under the work-incentive program for the city's 240,000 ADC and ADCU cases. Even though all the positions were filled, it amounted to only 4 percent of the total cases.

On the federal scene, while the details of the final welfare reform plan remain to be worked out, the work incentives as proposed by the President are similar to those recently implemented in New York. The national minimum welfare grant would be lower, however, and slightly different percentages of earnings could be retained with no reduction in welfare grants.

The fact that welfare is, in practice, such an accessible alternative to low-income work is troubling. No one knows the amount of income differential required to persuade substantial numbers of potentially employable welfare clients to depend on self-support rather than public assistance. To reduce arbitrarily the size of welfare grants to below equivalent minimum wage incomes would be socially unacceptable. Nor would it really help to increase minimum wages. Such a policy, in the words of a New York University study, "is likely to still further decrease the employment possibilities of unskilled people. It also adds incentives to employers to use more temporary help, hiring and firing as occasion demands, and thus worsening the likelihood of developing stable jobs and careers for poor people."

The optimum solution lies in the direction of putting the major emphasis, for employable males, on developing stable jobs with career ladders, so that husbands will be able better to support wives and children without going on welfare or resorting to abandonment. Even with the best-conceived job development program this will not happen overnight; supplementary payments would still have an important secondary role to play.

For those mothers who are genuinely separated, divorced, widowed, or unmarried, it is perhaps appropriate to reexamine the prevailing belief that they are entitled to welfare without being required to work. Of course, any change would have to be accompanied by a rational day-care program and other appropriate safeguards for the well-being of both mothers and children. However, most welfare mothers can work and many have done so.

In sum, employment, while by no means the total answer to the growing welfare burden, is certainly one of the keys to its solution. It would not immediately eliminate all the problems of child depend-

Previous Employment Experience of Welfare Mothers, April 1966	White, %	Nonwhite, %	Puerto Rican, %
Worked only before first child	52	33	28
Worked before and after	25	36	17
Worked only after first child	7	20	27
Total worked	84	89	72

ency, and obviously can have no more than a marginal impact on the aged or the disabled. However, it can begin to enable people and their families to help themselves rather than depend on a system which is not only extremely costly to the taxpayers, but also inadequate and ineffective as society's response to the poverty of our times.

NEW CUTTING EDGES AGAINST POVERTY

WHAT RESPONSE TO POVERTY?

The previous parts of this chapter highlight a number of crucial points. First, while the economic environment in New York City is relatively good, its structure is changing in such a way as to diminish the job prospects for the disadvantaged. And it was demonstrated that poverty remains a problem of striking dimensions, afflicting one or more out of every six families in the city.

Unfortunately, however, our knowledge of the problem does not give us the ability to solve it. Measured by the number of people it embraces and the number of dollars it spends, the public welfare system has constituted the major response to poverty in the city of New York. But all the billions spent on that program cannot mask the fact that, basically, it has not provided any solution. Indeed, Mitchell I. Ginsberg who, as former Human Resources Administrator, knew the New York City program only too well, is among its harshest critics, and has described the existing welfare system as being "bankrupt" as a social institution.

While there is general agreement about the perniciousness of the existing welfare approach to the problems of poverty, no unanimity exists concerning a better remedy. The spectrum of proposed substitutes such as guaranteed income, negative income tax, family allowances, and so on is extremely wide. A growing body of opinion, cutting across income and racial lines, holds that the very concept of grants from government to the poor, as a permanent ongoing arrangement, must be reexamined. Of course, for those who are too old, too ill, or too young, a better and more dignified form of social security than the present welfare system has to be found. But for those who

have the ability to work—or, more comprehensively, for all those who could be supported by an able breadwinner—the key to solving the problems of poverty may well be providing opportunities rather than handouts.

A more rational and uniform public welfare system such as those proposed by President Nixon and others may mitigate the evils that current programs inadvertently have created and may even ease some of the problems of poverty. By themselves, however, more money and improved systems will not be sufficient. By broadening the scope of public support for the nation's poor, the Nixon plan may intensify the problem of providing work incentives effective enough to move people off the welfare rolls. Certainly greater availability of more than marginally remunerative jobs to the economically handicapped is crucial for the success of any welfare reform.

THE PRIVATE SECTOR IS BECOMING INVOLVED The past few years have witnessed a surge of interest on the part of many corporations, community groups, and individuals in establishing vehicles to improve educational training and create better opportunities for individual and neighborhood advancement. Bridging the gap between promise and performance, however, too often has proven more difficult than any one imagined. In addition to money, clearly defined goals, strong dedication, and realistic action plans are all necessary ingredients for success in such endeavors.

Both individually and in consortia, the organizations listed below exemplify attempts to coordinate governmental, community, and business interests in a concerted drive to alleviate poverty and generally to improve the economy of the city.

New York Urban Coalition, involved in numerous programs, including one in which major business leaders actively work together with representatives of the local communities to develop indigenous businesses and economic growth in the ghettos. The coalition is also making efforts to improve the city's housing stock, and has devised programs for concentrated housing and retail-facilities development in a few selected neighborhoods.

Economic Development Council, consisting of prominent business leaders, including presidents and board chairmen of some of the largest banks and insurance, utility, and industrial companies in the nation, has been exploring ways to promote New York City's interests and optimize the development of its land and other economic resources. Specific major thrusts include working with public officials in the fields of welfare, job training, public safety, and the courts.

New York Public Development Corporations, in which leading businessmen have joined forces with the city for the purpose of developing space and facilities for industrial expansion.

Bedford-Stuyvesant Development and Service Corporation, a group of top business leaders assembled by the late Senator Robert F. Kennedy to work with the local community in vigorous job development, housing, education, and other socially directed programs. In conjunction with the Bedford-Stuyvesant Restoration Corporation, a black community-focused organization, some 45 new businesses and 1,200 jobs have been created and over $2 million loaned to community residents for mortgages and income improvements.

The Bedford-Stuyvesant experience offers another hopeful sign. In that section of Brooklyn, organized labor is cooperating with the local community in supervising and training community people to qualify for membership in the construction unions.

New York Chamber of Commerce, besides promoting economic development in the city, has put together a substantial consortium of private business for the purpose of training the disadvantaged for jobs.

Individual firms and private foundations, meanwhile, have participated in other programs. One of the most successful and significant areas has been the training and hiring of the hard-core unemployed. In the three years since the start of the program in 1968, 850 New York City companies, working individually and sometimes together, have contracted with the U.S. Department of Labor to train and hire people who could not find steady work or who lacked necessary job skills. To date, almost 50,000 people have been hired under the auspices of these training programs.

WHICH ENTREPRENEURS IN THE GHETTOS? Other strategies for economic development aim at strengthening the position of minority entrepreneurs within the ghettos. Some black and Puerto Rican leaders believe that the "instruments of capital" in their areas should be under minority ownership. They argue that their constituents make up an underdeveloped part of the American economy and will remain so—and, as such, poverty-prone—until they are able to build up a substantial entrepreneurial class and their own capital base.

The minority community is taking important steps to help itself. For example, the Puerto Rican Forum and the Puerto Rican Development Project both provide technical assistance to Puerto Rican businesses. The Puerto Rican Forum also guarantees loans and is helping local grocers in a buying cooperative. NEGRO (National Economic Growth and Reconstruction Organization) is a black self-help organization which aims to maximize employment and employee potential. Its several businesses, supported mostly by community shareholders, include a manufacturing plant, a construction company, and a hospital, as well as several community service operations.

Entrepreneurship among the minority groups, if successful, could turn out to be the most significant self-help program of all. Entrepreneurship, however, requires entrepreneurs, and these are not created overnight. They need accounting, financial, marketing, and other business skills which are not easily come by.

They also need capital for their business ventures. The first part of this is equity—the type that remains invested in the business but which could bring the investors unlimited profits over the years. On top of this there may be debt capital—the money temporarily borrowed from a bank or other lenders which must be repaid at fixed rates of interest. Too often, unfortunately, well-meaning proponents of minority capitalism look to lenders, rather than the equity investors, to provide all the capital, not realizing that man cannot live by debt alone, but that every business must be built on a solid base of equity.

Business is participating in the task of helping create a minority capital infrastructure not only through the New York Urban Coalition, but also independently or under the auspices of the Small Business Administration programs. That agency has responded to this need through both direct and guaranteed loans to minority business, presently flowing at a national rate of $200 million a year. Small Business Investment Corporations (SBICs) and Minority Enterprise Small Business Investment Corporations (MESBICSs), licensed by the SBA, can apply for funds from the SBA and provide both equity investments and other financial services to entrepreneurs. Funding by the Urban Coalition enabled the creation and operation of the Coalition Venture Corporation (CVC), which also provides money and services to minority businesses. Since its inception in 1969, CVC has put up $2 million for about 200 firms in the New York area.

The success of such ventures seems to depend on management expertise in both the lending and the spending functions. The very newness of this type of investment, however, has meant a slow, and often painful, learning process. One approach which has served to strengthen the entrepreneurship program has been for the financial lenders to provide purchase orders or encourage the local business community to give some of its business to minority entrepreneurs. Examples of this in New York are already occurring in such areas as computer software and food service. The federal government has also recognized the role it can play in buying from minority-owned firms. In fiscal 1970, about $55 million in procurement and service orders went from the Department of Defense, the Post Office, the General Services Administration, and the Department of Agriculture to minority businesses.

With full cooperation of not only the public and the private sectors, but also the minority communities themselves, such support techniques can succeed, provided their limitations are realized and careful attention is paid to the types of ventures selected. The American free-enterprise system is no longer kind to the small neighborhood store. And it is well to heed the advice of Michael Harrington, who points out that "there is no point in thinking that salvation will be found by making black men the small shopkeepers of poverty." A corollary of this is that minority entrepreneurs need not be restricted to ghetto areas, but might well seek to play a role in the economy at large.

"NEW" ROLES FOR BUSINESS   While well-conceived entrepreneurship among blacks and Puerto Ricans may create a capital base in the ghetto, which could, in time, constitute a major underpinning for ghetto economies, it is doubtful whether this approach, taken alone, is the complete answer to the poverty question. Moreover, it must be kept in mind that the economic "multiplier" effects of such undertakings might not be apparent for some time to come.

Clearly, job training is, and will remain, a major priority in any program designed to raise the income levels of the poor. Unfortunately, many people entering job-training programs all too often lack the schooling necessary for the more sophisticated jobs of today and tomorrow. To a large extent, the public school system is at fault in that it has not been properly responsive to the particular educational needs of the disadvantaged. Indeed, a strong case can be made that the education of those who will constitute the labor pool of the seventies and eighties is much too important to be entrusted entirely to educators of the traditional type. If business wishes to safeguard the quality of the education of its new workers, it will have to concern

itself much more closely than in the past with the entire education-training spectrum. This may well involve the private and public sectors working together to create a rational, functionally integrated education-training/employment system to replace the current hodge-podge of piecemeal and uncoordinated programs.

One example of shared educational responsibility in the formerly exclusively public realm is the Economic Development Council's program applied to four of New York City's high schools. EDC corporate members, working closely with the students, staff, and community groups, have provided full-time personnel to help attack some of these schools' problems. Assistance programs include job counseling, curriculum development, and business and operating advice (e.g., the use of computers to schedule classes).

Even if the education system were fully responsive to both the needs of all the students and the requirements of prospective employers, there would remain some people who, although able-bodied, might not be able to get jobs in the free labor market. The question with respect to this group then becomes whether there is a more creative alternative to public welfare grants. One proposed answer has been the host of generally nebulous government "youth" or "training" programs. While these may conceptually be one step better than welfare, they have already suffered more than their share of political and fiscal irregularity, all of which has led one black observer to comment that "the whole anti-poverty program is seen as a grand hustle for all involved."

Responding to the problems created by the scarcity of work skills among the disadvantaged, governments at all levels have created a proliferation of manpower training programs. An estimated $100 to $120 million is spent annually for such programs in New York City. After careful study, the Economic Development Council has characterized their overall pattern as "fragmented, over-lapping and duplicative, while at the same time inadequate for all important areas of need."[1] Apparently, public administration of manpower training programs has failed to achieve the desired results.

The idea of providing work training for those presumably able to absorb it is fundamentally sound. The problem is whether the administration of such programs might not better be contracted out to private business which, being economically rather than politically oriented, has a more inherent inclination to maximize efficiency, min-

[1] *New York City's Publicly-Financed Manpower Programs—Structure and Function,* Economic Development Council of New York City, Inc., Jan. 15, 1971.

51   Poverty and Economic Development

imize waste, and maintain the tightest possible fiscal controls. Some businesses are already administering such programs.

The extent of private-industry effort in the areas of education and poverty-program administration—to say nothing of physical building programs involving housing, factories, and offices—strongly suggests that it is business rather than government which can provide the most effective means for solving the problems of the poor. Some may question, however, whether this expanded function falls properly in the private sector's sphere of influence, and agree with Professor John Kenneth Galbraith, who has indicated that private industry is not genuinely interested in solving the problems of American cities.

This may well be true if business is expected to participate meaningfully without a profit incentive. For, as Senator Jacob K. Javits has pointed out: "You can't expect industry to carry on an unprofitable or nonprofitable business." The same point has been made trenchantly, if more earthily, by the president of MIND, Inc., which is in the business of developing human resources: "Whenever a human problem is solved, it's always because somebody has found a way to make a buck on it." Clearly, in order for the talent and ingenuity of business to be effectively harnessed, financial stimulus will have to be provided either directly or through appropriate tax incentives.

Under "normal" circumstances, a reasonable prospect for a satisfactory profit constitutes a sine qua non for private industry's engagement in any major undertaking. Nevertheless, that motivation is by no means the only reason for its active participation in significant programs to alleviate poverty in this or any other city. Put bluntly, enlightened business leaders are beginning to realize that performing an effective role in solving urban problems is the only way the free enterprise system will be able to survive in our society.

For example, G. William Miller, president of Textron, Inc., has pointed out:

> It's not very smart of business to pay the price twice; to pay it in terms of excess costs and also in terms of not being able to produce the goods or services which would be used by the disadvantaged if they were brought into the mainstream. . . . If private corporations are to fulfill their role . . . of making satisfactory return for shareholders on a continuing basis, then they are going to have to make investments today in human resources, just as they are making investments today in research or plants or market developments.

Unless business participates meaningfully in the struggle against domestic economic privation, it may well find its markets withering,

you give a damn
about the people
our ghettos,
wear this button.
Give a damn.
want a button, send your contribution with a self addressed, stamped envelope
York Urban Coalition, Box 5100, Grand Central Station, New York, N.Y. 10017
NAL DISTRICT
EXPERIEN
COUNT
NOV. 5.

its labor becoming scarce and less productive, and its profits eroded by rising tax burdens.

There are some things which private industry will not be able to do, such as making the kinds of value judgments which determine the type of society this nation will have. These will always remain the province of the people and their duly elected leaders at all levels from the President to the local community's officers. Nevertheless, business can be, and in numerous cases already is, a factor in the physical rehabilitation of the housing and other physical aspects of our disadvantaged areas. More pervasively, it may serve as the instrument (contractor) for the execution of programs to improve the overall socioeconomic status of our citizens, particularly those who live in poverty.

Just as our defense, outer-space, and other vast national programs are met by combining government control and funding with private business efficiency and imagination, so the problems of poverty—among the most difficult facing this nation today—might be solved by creatively harnessing together the best resources government and business have to offer.

Public Education in New York City

Low productivity is a factor of poverty, going hand in hand with poor education. It is widespread in every urban ghetto. Communities expect their educational system to help remedy this by building skills enabling individuals to work and produce effectively. But the community expects more from its educators than a narrow vocational training program. It wants its young to acquire a sense of values and some comprehesion of the nation's political and cultural heritage. And it looks to its schools as a force to relieve the frustrating pressures of ghetto life. So far, education has not fulfilled this role for reasons that are elusive and hard to unravel. Nor has the urban educational apparatus succeeded in upgrading itself to any substantial degree, despite huge increases in budget. What follows is an effort to get at some explanation for lapses in this area which spell the difference between social betterment and gross decay.

THE CITY, THE PEOPLE, AND THE SCHOOLS

New York City has a public school enrollment of 1.1 million pupils. This is larger than the entire population of such cities as Boston, St. Louis, San Francisco, or Pittsburgh. The city has 926 public schools, including 623 elementary, 154 junior and intermediate high schools, 65 academic high schools, 27 vocational high schools, and 46 special schools for socially maladjusted or handicapped children.

In the past two decades, the total population of the city has remained fairly stable, about 8 million. However, the composition has changed radically, with many of the relatively affluent moving out, while large numbers of newcomers—often poor and black or Puerto Rican—have come into New York. Those moving in tend to be young and to have larger families than those leaving the city.

Thus, two types of pressures bear on the public educational system. First, the number of school children has increased while the number of taxpayers to support this larger system through taxes has remained steady or even declined slightly.

POPULATION AND PUBLIC SCHOOL ENROLLMENT TRENDS IN NEW YORK CITY, 1950–1970

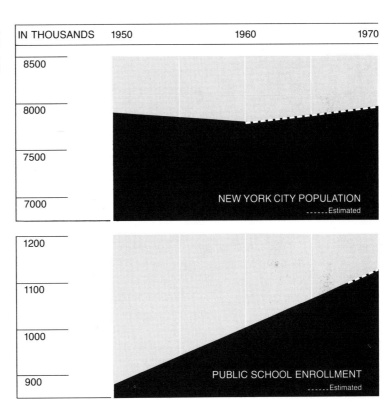

Second, the ethnic composition of the pupil population has changed much more than that of the population at large. While the percentage of blacks and Puerto Ricans in New York City's population has risen from about 20 to roughly 35 percent during the past decade, the percentage of these two groups in the public school population has climbed from 33 to about 60 percent. The number of Puerto Rican and black pupils has doubled in the past 10 years, while the number of white pupils is one-fourth lower than it was in the early sixties.

The changing ethnic patterns in the schools have been quite uneven in terms of their geographical distribution throughout the city. The outmigration of whites has been most pronounced in the past few years in Brooklyn and the Bronx, while Queens and Richmond have maintained their predominately white profile. In Manhattan, the sharp losses of white students have continued, particularly on the east side of the island.

A great deal of potential pressure is removed from the public schools by the parochial and private schools where about two-fifths (or 350,000) of New York City's white children receive their education. The percentage of black children in nonpublic schools is infinitesimally small. As for Puerto Rican children, there are indications that they have begun to enter parochial schools in the central city in increasing numbers.

THE SYSTEM'S STRUCTURE

The New York City Board of Education has been responsible for the city's public schools since about the turn of the century, when the five boroughs—and their educational systems—were consolidated and their administration centralized. The board's mission is to run elementary, intermediate, academic, vocational, and other schools and classes necessary to meet the education needs and demands of the city.

The school system employs over 100,000 people. This accounts for some 30 percent of New York City's aggregate civil service payroll. The bulk of these (almost 60,000) are teachers. An additional 8,000 are in supervisory and other noninstructional categories. About 6,000 are in administrative positions, and the remaining full- and part-time employees provide custodial, school-lunch, and other supporting services.

New York City has thirty-one community school districts, established on the basis of average daily attendance at each of the elementary and junior high–intermediate schools. There are six districts in Manhattan, six in the Bronx, eleven in Brooklyn, seven in Queens, and one in Richmond. Each community district has a nine-member, elected community board with authority to administer the elementary and junior high–intermediate schools, select community superintendents, and appoint and assign teachers. The Board of Education retains jurisdiction over high schools and special schools and classes.

FUNDING THE SCHOOLS: INCOME SOURCES

Over the past decade, the budget for education and related activities[1] has risen from $594 million in 1960–61 to about $1,870 million in 1970–71, representing a 215 percent increase. Education in New York State is financed by a combination of locally collected taxes (largely property taxes) and state aid. The amount of state aid is inversely proportional to a school district's relative economic ability to support education, with some extra allowances permitted for population density and other factors.

Although New York City has thirty-one regular school districts, until 1967 the city was considered as one school district when applying for funds from New York State. Because the assessed property valuation was so high, New York City received only the minimum flat grant of $238 per pupil from the state. In 1967, the legislation was changed to allow New York City to compute its aid formula on the basis of the property-valuation figure for each of its five boroughs, which led to increased state aid. New York City has also received additional money ($48 million in 1970–71) from a State Urban Aid fund established by the legislature in 1968 to deal with educational needs of the disadvantaged.

Within New York City, funds for education come not only from real estate taxes, but also from general fund revenues. These include monies gathered from sales taxes and income taxes as well as other miscellaneous sources.

In 1960, real estate taxes provided 56.3 percent of the total tax levy in New York; in 1970–71, 48.6 percent of the funds came from real estate. In both instances, the difference has been supplied from general fund revenues. The need for revenues from additional sources stems from the fact that all expenditures have risen much more than the assessed property valuation in New York City.

Most educators have long recognized the need for strong injections of state and federal funds to help defray the rising costs of education, especially in those areas where a heavy burden rests on real estate revenues. As the costs of other urban services increase, general fund revenues are often insufficient to cover all needs. During the first half of the sixties, New York City provided about two-thirds of the total funds for education and the state about one-third. Federal funds contributed less than 1 percent toward the support of increased general education costs.

---

[1] These figures include the costs of related health services, public utilities, and debt service in addition to the direct expenses of the Board of Education.

Title I of the Elementary and Secondary Education Act (ESEA) of 1965 provided for federal funding to qualifying schools for special compensatory programs, assuming that the ongoing costs and programs funded as described above were continued. This was to ensure a maintenance of effort by New York City and New York State. Generally, public and private schools are eligible for Elementary and Secondary Education Act (ESEA) funds if 50 percent or more of the students are reading at least one year below grade level in the fifth grade or two or more years below in the eighth grade or beyond. New York City easily meets these requirements. In 1970, over 30 centralized Title I projects were operated by the Board of Education itself, at a cost of $52 million. School districts utilized an additional $13.5 million to operate their own projects.

USES OF FUNDS

Since 1960–61, school expenditures have climbed over 200 percent, while the number of pupils in the system has increased only 16 percent. The large growth in per capita costs and expenditures reflects surges in personnel and services, substantial jumps in various administrative and support costs, and higher teachers' salaries.

In the 1970–71 budget, the average expenditures per pupil were approximately $608 in the regular elementary schools, $877 in the regular intermediate schools, $777 in the academic high schools, and $1,182 in the vocational high schools. The averages, however, are deceptive and mask wide divergences which may run anywhere from about $600 to over $1,700 when other items such as health care and transportation are included.

Aside from differences in school organization, much of the variation in costs is attributable to the range of salaries for teachers with different levels of experience. Schools (with mostly white enrollments) having large numbers of teachers with long service have high operating costs. The range of teacher salaries in the fall of 1970 was from $8,450 to $16,000, and progression along the wage schedule took eight years. Teachers are eligible for retirement pay after twenty years of service and 45 years of age.

THE PUBLIC SCHOOL SYSTEM: PROVIDER OF EDUCATIONAL SERVICES TO SOCIETY

In spite of the increased resources which have been directed to education in New York City, criticism of the city's schools is widespread. Citizens are probably more sensitive about education than any other service they "buy" from the public sector with their tax dollars. They feel that if basic functions such as education are not properly performed, the whole rationale for men to live in organized taxpaying units is called into question.

It is well to remember that until recently the New York City school system was generally acclaimed as the showcase of the nation. Since the inception of its consolidated school system, the city has been a leader in innovation in education. It was among the first to recognize the need to provide education appropriate to its varied ethnic strains, as typified by the early neighborhood schools which often took on many of the customs of the community. The city also geared educational resources to the economic needs of the times. It provided continuing and evening education for those who did not plan to go on to college.

Rising costs—and taxes—related to the schools are, however, running into taxpayer resistance. These taxpayers, whether they be individuals who live in New York City or businesses which depend largely on the city for their labor supply, might well be more amenable to supporting education if they were assured that the system was doing the job for which it was intended. This is equally true for public transportation or any other urban service, where the price that thoughtful citizens are willing to pay is based on the efficacy and quality of the service.

A number of educational authorities suggest that the mission of an education system is to pass on the accumulation of knowledge and in so doing to seek the maximum development of an individual's ability and equip him to deal with the changing demands of the modern world. This involves a number of objectives, from mastery of conventional tools such as reading and numbers manipulation to the somewhat more elusive—but equally critical—behavioral goals. At the same time, the student should be taught how to learn, because the world of the eighties and nineties may require skills only dimly perceived on the threshold of the seventies.

These objectives are difficult to attain even where all segments of the society have common expectations. However, the educational and cultural backgrounds and aspirations of the various ethnic strains prominent in New York City today differ quite widely, and in some respects are even more diffuse than those of the groups most prevalent in previous decades. The New York labor market, moreover, has also changed, becoming increasingly white-collar-oriented. Public education must adapt to these two realities.

Given the costs of education, it is legitimate for New York's people and businesses to ask how well the present school system meets the city's changing needs. If more money must be spent on education, as appears inevitable, in which areas will these investments be most effective? It is against the background of questions such as these that businessmen, who might normally be considered as outsiders with respect to education, must inquire into the process and explore how their tax monies are being spent.

ELEMENTARY SCHOOLS

THE SCHOOLS AND THE DISADVANTAGED

The education of the disadvantaged in the nation's public schools was treated at length in *Equality of Educational Opportunity*, published under the auspices of the Department of Health, Education and Welfare and generally known as the Coleman Report. Although there has been criticism of the report, the detailed research it represents has not as yet been undertaken in any other study. It found that, when economically disadvantaged children began school with an initial skill deficiency, the gap between their achievement and that of their advantaged peers widened, rather than narrowed, as the children progressed through school. The most important variables associated with achievement were the socioeconomic backgrounds of the pupils themselves. Traditional school inputs (teacher characteristics, school facilities, per capita costs, to name a few) were found to have a relatively small impact on achievement levels.

Elementary education is thus a focal point in any attempt to compensate for educational disadvantage.[1] Failure to have mastered skills in the early grades too often leads to a continued pattern of failure, whereby both the children and the educators unwittingly expect and thus reinforce earlier deficiencies in achievement.[2]

One might ask whether the propositions of the Coleman Report apply to New York City, and what possible roles socioeconomic factors and school inputs play in learning. While learning has many dimensions, the only measure generally available throughout New York City's elementary and junior high schools (and in the public domain) are the Metropolitan Achievement Test (MAT) scores. Unfortunately, MAT scores quantify only reading and vocabulary knowledge. Therefore, they may suffer from cultural bias, inasmuch as their frame of reference is generally the white-middle-class value system to which inner-city children cannot easily relate.[3]

[1] Indeed, there are those who suggest that the "pre-school" ages are the most important (e.g., "Why Some 3-Year Olds Get A's—And Some Get C's" by Maya Pines in *The New York Times Magazine*, July 6, 1969).

[2] See Robert Rosenthal and Lenore Jacobson, "Pygmalion in the Classroom," *The Urban Review*, September 1968.

[3] See, for example, Miriam Wasserman, "Planting Pansies on the Roof," *The Urban Review*, January 1969.

We are obliged to look at reading scores, keeping in mind that, to the extent that words like "chittlin" and "hustle" do not feature as prominently on the test as "boat," "lake," and "elm," the test is "rigged" in favor of children who are white and/or relatively well-off and against children who are black and/or poor.[1] Despite the shortcomings in the design and administration of the tests, however, there is no agreed-upon substitute measure of output.

The Metropolitan Achievement Tests are given in April of each year. The "normal" achievement level of each grade is the number of years and months (one school year equals ten months) that a student in that grade has been in school. Thus, for a fourth grader, the normal reading level is 4 years and 7 months (4.7) when tested in April; for a fifth grader, 5 years and 7 months (5.7). The pupils are tested against other pupils in large metropolitan areas. The reading level used in this report is the average of the scores on the word-knowledge and paragraph-meaning parts of the test.

In 1968, less than half of New York City's students were reading at or above grade level. Slightly over one of every three fifth graders was reading one or more years below grade level; one in seven was reading two or more years below grade.

In the city's 557 elementary schools for which data were available,[2] there was great variation in the average fifth grade reading scores— from a low of 3.6 (more than two years behind grade) for a school in the predominately Puerto Rican South Bronx to the highest score of 8.5 (almost three years above grade) for a school in "suburban" eastern Queens. Needless to say, variations in scores among individual pupils were much broader.

A statistical test was conducted to see how the following variables related to achievement (measured by fifth grade MAT):[3]

1. Percentage of white students
2. Average daily attendance

[1] However, Martin Meyer argues that "'Chittlin' tests which supposedly reward the sort of knowledge common in the slums are essentially useless because later surrender value of such knowledge is so slight." *The Urban Review,* February 1969.

[2] This excludes the More Effective Schools (MES), which are discussed separately beginning on page 72.

[3] The stepwise multiple regression used all available variables from the new Program Budgeting reporting system, on a school-by-school basis. Clearly, both the scope and quality of the raw data pertaining to both the independent and dependent variables leave much to be desired and thus lead to no hard and fast conclusions. Nevertheless, it is submitted that analyses based on actual numbers, imperfect as they may be, constitute a useful complement to most other evaluations of the schools based largely on highly selective facts or impressions.

3. Percentage of students receiving free lunches (poverty index)
4. Percentage of permanently licensed teachers
5. Degree of building utilization
6. Rate of pupil mobility (annual admissions and discharges as a percent of average daily attendance)

The analysis attempted to measure the importance of these factors to the reading scores. Taken together, the variables accounted for almost three-fourths of the variation in reading scores. The factors most highly associated with higher achievement levels are a large percentage of white students and, to a smaller extent, a high attendance level and a small percentage of pupils eating free lunch—considered by some to be a poverty index.

In other words, in New York City, as in the nation (according to the Coleman Report), middle-class children, predominately white, do better than children from lower socioeconomic strata, which contain large numbers of minority-group people. The traditional school inputs as measured here play a relatively minor role in relation to achievement.

Absolute reading levels, by themselves, are deficient in that they reflect a static condition at a single point in time. To look at the effect on education a little more closely, the amount of improvement from one grade to the next may be a more important measure of achievement. The average improvement from the fourth grade in 1967 to the fifth grade in 1968 was 1 year and 1 month (1.1). However, when the same variables used to predict the actual fifth-grade score are used in a regression to estimate the improvement from one year to the next, relatively little correlation exists. Most of such correlation as does exist is due to the influence of the racial variable. Some other variables also correlate positively, but quite weakly. The individual factors associated with the absolute level of achievement do not seem strongly related to the improvement in scores.

There were 150 schools (excluding MES) where 10 percent or less of the student population was white (the rest being black and Puerto Rican). In these schools the average fifth-grade reading score (1968) was 4 years and 6 months (4.6), and the average improvement from the fourth to fifth grade was 9 months. By comparison, in the 407 schools (excluding MES) where the racial composition was greater than 10 percent white, the average fifth-grade reading score was 6 years and 3 months and the average improvement 1 year and 2 months. Comparisons between the black/Puerto Rican and the other schools for the different variables are indicated in the table.

Averages	Black/Puerto Rican Schools*	Other Schools†
Reading score (fifth grade)	4.6 years‡	6.3 years
Change in score	.9 years	1.2 years
Permanent staff	62%	72%
School utilization	102%	87%
Free lunch	54%	21%
Attendance	87%	90%
Mobility	42%	24%

*Defined as at least 90 percent Black or Puerto Rican.
†Defined as less than 90 percent Black or Puerto Rican.
‡One year = 10 months.

Even among 150 black/Puerto Rican schools, the average figures mask some very notable differences. For example, 24 schools in this group registered an average improvement of 1.5 years.

For the 150 black/Puerto Rican schools, as with the total New York City universe, quantitative measures of pupil or school characteristics did not correlate in any substantial way with the change in reading scores, except if the absolute reading level itself was taken as an independent variable.

Predominately Puerto Rican schools appear to have about the same scores as predominately black schools. Non-English-speaking pupils are informally evaluated on a scale of A to F for fluency in English. C is the minimal fluency for regular class assignment, but students are included in the regular testing program only at the discretion of the teacher. There were approximately 110,400 children in the city school system in 1967–68 who were evaluated as C, D, E, or F on the fluency scale. In grades kindergarten through six, 81,400 pupils, or about 13 percent of the elementary school enrollment, have been evaluated in reading from C to F.

In 1968, New York City employed about 175 teachers of English as a second-language; not all of them were full-time staff members. Some critics assert that the number of teachers and the time available for instruction are inadequate to provide education for the number of non-English-speaking children.

MONEY AND OUTPUT Expenditures for each school include the amount of New York City and New York State money allocated to the school (exclusive of funds for capital improvements) and money from federal aid, primarily funds under Title I and other provisions of the Elementary and Secondary Education Act. Per capita costs in the 150 schools with enrollments 90 percent or more black and Puerto Rican averaged $839 in 1967–68, ranging from a low of $529 per pupil to a high of $1,560.

Regardless of the variations in socioeconomic characteristics of the students in these 150 schools, there is no statistical correlation between the aggregate amounts of money spent per pupil and the improvement in reading scores from the fourth to the fifth grades. In other words, in these 150 schools, preliminary evidence does not appear to indicate that an expenditure of one amount is any more effective in changing a pupil's level of achievement than an expenditure of another.

The lack of correlation in black/Puerto Rican schools between changes in achievement and the absolute level of quantitative factors such as higher-salaried experienced teachers or school equipment (as indicated by per capita cost figures) raises the question of whether or not continued indiscriminate funding of these items will in itself necessarily increase educational output proportionately.

An interesting case in point is the More Effective Schools (MES) program. MES offered a particularly intensive combination of resources to prevent and compensate for academic failure. The twenty-seven schools in the MES program in 1970–71 provided a host of supportive and innovative services to the children. For example, class size was reduced to a maximum of twenty in kindergarten and twenty-two in grades one through six. Extra teachers were made available as well as guidance and medical services. The objectives of MES were to enhance reading and math skills as well as to increase pupil interest in education, promote higher staff morale, and incorporate parent interest into the educational process.

In addition to MES, the Special Service Schools program was established to compensate for educational disadvantage, and, on the average, the two programs serviced essentially the same type of students in terms of racial and poverty characteristics. Using the basic data from earlier analyses, the average poverty level in the Special Service Schools is 55 percent, while in MES it is 58 percent. The percentage of white students averages about 16 percent in the Special Service Schools, while they comprise 19 percent of the enrollment in MES. (The poverty level for regular elementary schools is 13 percent, and the average white enrollment is 75 percent.)

The table shows the estimated cost per pupil, the improvement in reading scores, and the "cost for each month of improvement" (dividing total cost by the number of months of improvement). The regular elementary schools serve a more "advantaged" group of students, and no genuine comparisons can be made between the achievements of these schools and the Special Service or More Effective Schools.

However, since both Special Service and MES reach essentially the same type of student body, some crude cost comparisons between them can be set forth in a very tentative and approximate sense.

Cost and Achievement Comparisons

	Estimated cost per pupil	Change from 4th to 5th grade reading score, years	Cost per month of change
Regular day elementary Schools	$ 790	1.2	$ 66
Special Service Schools	$ 887	.9	$ 99
More Effective Schools	$1,200	1.0	$120

Data for 1967–68, Executive Budget. Calculated from available data for 325 regular elementary, 232 Special Service Schools, and 20 More Effective Schools, academic year 1967–68. One year = 10 months.

Using costs and scores in 1967–68, the More Effective Schools cost almost 35 percent more per pupil than the Special Service Schools.[1] The improvement in reading scores was also greater in MES than in the Special Service Schools. The MES children had a 1.0 year improvement from 1967 to 1968; the Special Service children, 9 months. However, it might be argued that New York City was paying an additional 35 percent to get one more month of achievement (in terms of test scores). Stated slightly differently, in the Special Service Schools, each month of improvement cost about $99; in MES, each month cost $120. Achievement is very important, but it is legitimate to ask at this point whether or not the "output" justifies the cost.

THE ROLE OF QUALITY Good education, like any other service, needs adequate funding. The appropriate question is not how much expenditures will be increased, but to which inputs monies will be directed. In a sample group of fourteen black/Puerto Rican schools, each principal was interviewed to see if his attitudes about the roles of administrative and teaching staffs correlated in any way with the improvements in reading. A "school quality index" was derived, and seems to explain 74 percent of variation in reading score improvement in the sample.

Significant improvements in reading skills were associated with a principal's belief that he had a competent professional staff in the fourth and fifth grades, respected his teachers' aides working in the

[1]As indicated earlier, the spread in costs between these two programs has jumped to about 50 percent. Preliminary analysis of a sample of 1969 scores suggests that costs per month of achievement remain substantially higher in MES than in Special Service Schools.

classroom and used them extensively, had meaningful parent and community involvement in the school, and practiced or supported innovative administrative or teaching techniques. Relative backsliding in achievement was associated with opposite attitudes.

Even if the high coefficient of correlation is discounted somewhat because of the subjectivity necessarily involved in translating attitudes (qualitative) into a numerical index (quantitative), the resulting numbers appear to be, at the least, provocative.

Two elements appear to be at work in those schools that yielded the high correlations. First of all, a school that manages to involve the total environment of the child into the education process has more resources, both tangible and intangible, available for education than a school that does not. Secondly, for a combination of these factors to be operating, the staff, the community, and the children must have respect for themselves and the other participants in the school.

It is increasingly apparent that children with educational disadvantages need a multitude of services to help compensate for a heritage of poverty. Every resource available to the school should be used to educate the child to learn how to learn. This means significant parent and community involvement working with and helping those entrusted with the education of their children. It goes without saying that communication and flexibility are key responses for all groups concerned.

The role of the children themselves should not be understated. Many educational authorities believe that children can perform more constructively in furthering their own education. In particular, some children may well have the ability to teach or help teach others, and such opportunities should be explored and utilized.

Nor should the purely physical factors be neglected. To be sure, the evidence appears to suggest that reductions in class size and physical structuring (whether it be in the form of full-fledged educational parks or simply a program to relieve overcrowding) can be negated by shortcomings in instructional quality. Nevertheless, for best results, improvements in quality of principals, teachers, etc., should be accompanied by improved physical conditions in the schools, reductions in class size where appropriate, and other quantitative measures.

All this will take money, and there is no question that the education system needs a great deal of it, especially in view of the great payoff for society from the right investments in quality education.

Originally, elementary schools were organized for students in grades one through eight, and completion of the eighth grade was marked by a graduation ceremony. For many, this marked the end of formal education. The changing demands of a technical society, in conjunction with more stringent child labor laws and mandatory increases in the number of years a child had to remain in school, resulted in an increased high school enrollment. The response of the high schools was to provide more varied curricula, often geared to the special vocational needs of those who planned to go immediately to work.

Intermediate (junior) high schools were popularized in New York during the 1920s, and included grades seven through nine. Educators recognized the need for an institution to provide an academic and emotional transition between elementary and secondary education. However, the junior high school came into being only after intensive labor pains, for neither the elementary nor the high schools wished to relinquish control to the junior highs. In many ways, the organization and prestige of the junior high schools still reflect their earlier "stepchild" status.

Enrollment in the junior and academic high schools stood at 232,485 and 246,078, respectively, in 1970-71. This represented increases of 25 and 30 percent, respectively, since 1960-61. In 1971, 62 percent of the junior high school students and 48 percent of those in the academic high schools were black and Puerto Rican.

In the vocational high schools, enrollment at 39,093 in 1970-71 had remained fairly constant over the decade. About 67 percent of the vocational students were black and Puerto Rican. Vocational education is designed, too often, to provide graduates with specific, generally blue-collar skills, in a labor market that is increasingly white-collar- and service-occupation-oriented.

In 1964, the Allen Report recommended that the existing academic and vocational high schools be reorganized and combined into comprehensive high schools, which would enable students to select among different curricula, or elements thereof, while attending the same schools. In addition, the comprehensive high school plan would eliminate the general diploma, provide more intensive guidance, and enable a child to choose a vocational curriculum in the eleventh or twelfth grade, rather than the tenth grade as at present. The board has had plans for several years, but administrative and construction delays have slowed the implementation process.

Comprehensive high schools would incorporate grades nine through twelve, and the junior or intermediate highs would then take over grades five through eight, with the first four years of school undertaken in the elementary structure.

Although there are no universally acceptable or complete figures to indicate the number of high school dropouts, some knowledgeable persons estimate that two-fifths or more of those who enter high school do not complete it. This figure would closely correspond to the percentage of children who are reading two or more years below grade level in the ninth grade.

Traditionally, the predominant way of grouping students is by "tracking," whereby children of similar achievement levels are kept in the same class. Children rarely move from low to high tracks, and low achievement in elementary school appears to be conducive to the same pattern in junior high and later in senior high school. Intermediate school graduates are placed in high school programs (i.e., general as opposed to academic) on the basis of their third-term marks in the ninth grade (or eighth), and classes are established in the late spring without necessarily consulting with the pupils themselves. Low-achieving pupils are put into the general or commercial diploma course, from which it is difficult to shift to an academic course. To be sure, reading scores of many high school students look dismal, but greater flexibility in class placement, etc., might help to bring previously untapped intellectual potential to the surface.

Graduation with an academic diploma indicates the successful passing of specified New York State Regents examinations and is a basic credential for college admission. In 1969, 51 percent of the graduates from the regular academic high schools received such diplomas. This figure would be considerably smaller if the pupils who dropped out of school had remained until graduation.

Graduates with a general diploma have fulfilled less rigorous course requirements (for example, general math rather than algebra). Some observers refer to the general diploma cynically as a "certificate of attendance." Black and Puerto Rican children account for a disproportionately high percentage of such diplomas. In three regular academic high schools where two-thirds or more of the graduates received only general diplomas, enrollments were predominately black and Puerto Rican (ranging from 75 to over 96 percent). The three schools with the lowest percentages of general diploma graduates were schools with predominately white enrollments (75 percent or more). The ninth and tenth grade reading scores in the three schools with a high ratio of general diplomas were also significantly below average, with the scores averaging almost three years below normal achievement.

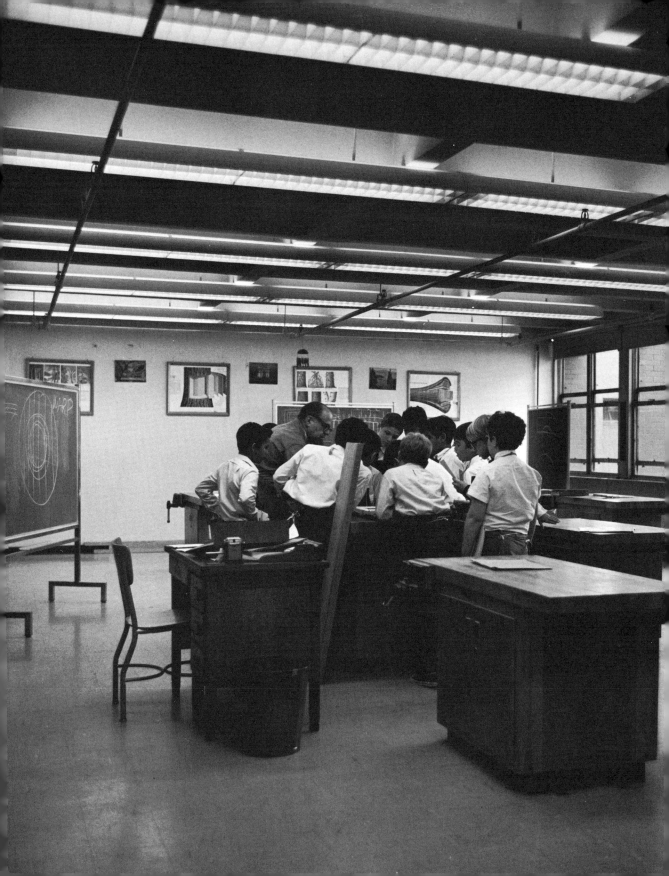

Learning problems are aggravated in many cases by general malaise which has its origins in larger problems facing the society and the nation as a whole. In the high schools, as in the colleges, these feelings have contributed to some measure of unrest, particularly when the students feel that their aspirations are being thwarted by "the Establishment."

The prevalence of narcotics in a number of high schools and even some junior highs also affects the school climate. While no official records are kept, unofficial estimates place the percentage of drug users (primarily marijuana and heroin) at nearly 40 percent of student enrollments at some schools, with perhaps 20 percent of the users afflicted with severe addiction problems.

COSTS The 1969–79 Executive Budget of the Mayor allocated $543 million of the $1.2 billion designated for instruction costs in all schools to intermediate and high schools. The estimated comprehensive cost per pupil for 1969–70 was $970 in the regular intermediate schools, $1,070 in the Special Service Intermediate Schools, $1,268 in the academic high schools, and $1,798 in the vocational high schools. In addition, a few specialized but small high school programs operate at costs of over $2,000 a student.

The significantly higher costs of vocational education are probably attributable to lower pupil-teacher ratios (about $16\frac{1}{2}:1$ in vocational versus $21:1$ in academic) and higher operating costs for instructional equipment. In view of the instances of mismatch between much of the vocational schooling and new job opportunities, it is questionable whether all these large expenditures can be justified in terms of either the economic and vocational needs of New York City or the value of this education to the student himself.

For the future, financial pressures will come not only from operating costs, but also from capital costs, which are slated to rise substantially. High school construction has lagged severely behind needs. In academic high schools, average enrollments are more than 130 percent of capacity, with several schools operating at close to 175 percent of capacity, resulting in double or triple sessions. The vocational highs are not as crowded, but generally operate at about capacity.

WHERE DOES THE SCHOOL SYSTEM GO FROM HERE?

MANAGING BY RESULTS— AND THE DECENTRALIZATION QUESTION

The preceding inquiry into the schools leaves some doubt about whether or not resources are being allocated most efficiently and results are commensurate with money spent.

It might be argued in defense of the existing system that various new programs require more time (and more funds) to reach their full potential. However, it appears that some ghetto schools which have been staffed by high-quality principals and teachers have shown significant improvements in relatively brief spans of time.

Perhaps, therefore, more attention should be given to the selection and evaluation of principals and teachers for the disadvantaged. This might include a review of the examinations for the key policy posts of principal and assistant principal, presently supervised by the Board of Examiners. Successful passage of these exams depends more often than not on memorization of extensive materials regarded by some as "trivia," and coaching courses abound to enable one to pass the exam. Critics assert that these exams have never been adequately scrutinized by independent testing consultants and claim that there is no evidence that the exams measure a candidate's administrative, teaching, or factual ability. Under the decentralization legislation effective July 1970, local school boards could use other means to select teachers in schools which rank in the bottom 40 percent of the city in reading ability. New procedures are also being instituted for the selection of principals.

One might argue that the most important attribute of a principal or teacher should not be whether he is liked by his superiors, his peers, or even the community, but whether he is able to elicit satisfactory improvement from the children he teaches.[1] Might it not make sense that allocations of funds (and the question of centralization/decentralization) should follow from this basic principle?

It might be worthwhile for federal and city educational authorities to explore whether or not Title I and other monies could be put to good advantage by providing principals of disadvantaged schools with discretionary funds to use for whatever special purposes they themselves deem necessary to improve achievement levels in their schools. Thus, some principals may emphasize smaller class sizes; others might hire remedial reading teachers or aides; others may concentrate on teacher training; others might invest in audio-visual aids; while others may place emphasis on special courses and activities for parents and other community members. As part of this overall concept, the principals involved would also have a certain amount of discretionary authority with respect to curriculum (e.g., additional time as well as

---

[1] The most recent United Federation of Teachers contract makes reference, although in generalized and vague terms, to the need to develop "objective criteria of professional accountability" for teachers.

staff for teaching English to non-English-speaking children). The critical point is that decisions on special funds, curriculum adjustments, etc., and the ultimate accountability for the effectiveness of the monies and programs would be concentrated in the same person—namely, the principal.

In sum, the principal would be given the funds and the freedom to succeed and be held accountable for results. On this point the Committee for Economic Development has recently suggested that "the schools be held accountable for their product. Special educational programs for the disadvantaged should be funded only where evaluations have been designed to identify concrete results and the conditions necessary for achieving those results."[1]

To be sure, this is easier said than done. Measuring achievement even in subjects such as reading and math is still not an exact science. Moreover, how would achievement of behavioral goals be evaluated? And what would "accountability" really involve once "objective criteria" are developed? Would inadequate teachers and principals, particularly in disadvantaged schools, be transferred out or even removed? Would teachers whose students achieve outstanding results be appropriately rewarded? And if so, by some sort of special money bonus, or would they just be given nonmonetary incentives?

It does seem that if "accountability" attains a position of preeminent importance in the schools, it may well be that neither total centralization nor total decentralization is called for. The definition of the broad overall objectives of education and the consequent establishment of criteria call for a certain amount of standardization and uniformity. Nevertheless, the educational philosophers and those devising and administering tests must be sensitive to the realities of the school population in terms of race, poverty, etc.

In setting specific target levels for improvement in each area of study in each school, if this approach be used, the central board might oversee the process which would fundamentally be undertaken by teams consisting of the local board, district superintendent, and principal of the school in question. This is no simple matter in practice. Even after three years of a planning-programming-budgeting system, the Board of Education still lacks the detailed operational data which are a prerequisite for any rational setting of targets for individual pupils or even individual classes or schools.

Meanwhile, it might be logical if details of inputs into "disad-

[1] *Education for the Urban Disadvantaged*, Committee for Economic Development, 1971.

vantaged" schools were handled at the most decentralized professional level—the principal. The principal, in turn, needs to elicit and win the support of the local community if he is to be successful in achieving his overall mission. The community must be drawn into close cooperation with the principal in guiding and promoting the education of its children.

POTENTIAL ROLES FOR BUSINESS The interest of business in education is threefold:

First, every factor which affects the environment has a decided impact on business. This could be the purity of the air, the efficiency of the transportation system, or the quality of education.

Second, since most students eventually go into the working world, potential employers have the greatest amount to gain—or lose—by the quality of the educational process. Every enlightened businessman realizes that the student of today is the employee of tomorrow and will directly determine the ability of his company to accomplish its own objectives.

Third, business, through the tax system, might be considered a major underwriter of public education, and thus has an interest, if not an obligation, in making sure that funds for education are spent most effectively.

A number of problems faced by the schools are essentially similar to problems which businesses successfully deal with on a day-to-day basis. For instance, sound business thinking could well be applied to the problems of school overcrowding in order to devise the most efficient allocation of time and space so as to minimize the overcrowding. More generally, business could provide meaningful assistance in cost-effectiveness education.

Most pertinent of all is the role that private industry can and should play in establishing a link between the high schools and the world of work. Such an involvement, at a minimum, might consist of career guidance, placement assistance, and some measure of work-study programs.

In order for business to be truly effective, however, there should be a radical change in its role vis-à-vis the high schools. In New York City, up to this point, the major business involvement in the high schools has been through the vocational education programs, which are largely blue-collar-oriented and thus relate to a shrinking section in the city's economy. It would seem to make sense to reorient our concept of vocational education more toward white-collar training rather than to some of the conventional manual skills.

Planning for the future, companies with corporate head offices in New York City, accountants and those providing other business services, and the real estate, insurance, banking, and finance industry spokesmen should help devise specific programs jointly with the public school authorities for high school vocational training. These could involve such things as joint curriculum planning and teacher training. The specific programs would have to be on a scale relevant to the anticipated employment needs of the respective industries. The essence of the idea is to establish a link between what the youngster is doing in the high school and the type of job available to him upon completion of his education.

More broadly, business has a role constantly to reexamine the public educational system in an objective, dispassionate way; to explore how resources are being used; and to promote improvements for the benefit of the schools, their pupils, and society as a whole.

PRESCHOOL PROGRAMS

In New York City, preschool programs[1] of all types serve approximately 163,000 children from ages 2 to 5, double the number of a decade ago. The bulk of the growth stems from kindergarten and prekindergarten programs in the city schools, Head Start by the Community Development Agency, and the inauguration of programs by other interested groups.

Preschool Programs in New York City. 1970

Program	Number of Children	Percent
Kindergarten, public	95,000	58
Prekindergarten, public	9,400	6
Head Start, full year	5,900	4
Head Start, summer	17,800	11
Other *	35,000	21
Total	163,100	100

*These include parochial schools, social, community, and philanthropic organizations, private schools, voluntary agencies, colleges, hospitals, cooperatives, and proprietary nursery schools.

PRESCHOOL UNDER THE MICROSCOPE

The few programs in New York which have been comprehensively evaluated have shown inconclusive results as to the return on investment. One factor hindering effective preschool evaluation is the diffi-

[1]Defined by the Health Department as six or more children enrolled in a program which meets at least five hours a week and more than a month per year. The service can be known as a child-care center, day nursery, day-care agency, nursery school, kindergarten, or play school, or by any other name.

culty involved in constructing adequate instruments to test very young children, often from widely diversified backgrounds. A further contributing factor is the inadequacy of financial support for thorough appraisal.

As a case in point, the recent nationwide evaluation of Head Start centers (including one in New York City) by Westinghouse Learning Corporation (April 1969) asserted that there were relatively small increases in cognitive ability after the full-year remedial program. The validity of the data has been challenged, however, by experts who question the sampling and testing methods on which these conclusions are based.

However, a number of small experiments have been conducted with both average and disadvantaged young children, with testing of groups carefully controlled. In some of the programs, notably those conducted by Dr. Martin Deutsch, Director of the Institute for Development Studies in New York City, substantial gains in scholastic achievement over a period of years have been found.

One eventually must face the question of priorities. Given present funding, there exists a temptation among even most knowledgeable authorities to parcel out portions for sporadic attempts to upgrade scattered groups of preschoolers. Dr. Martin Deutsch describes the situation as follows:

> There is tremendous pressure to set up programs without adequate preparation and training of teachers and without a well-developed curriculum. I think that greater immediate emphasis should be placed on universal kindergarten, with reduced pupil-teacher ratio.[1]

TRYING TO EQUATE SUPPLY AND DEMAND

When proven techniques are applied to excessively large groups of seriously deprived children, the results indicate that, at the preschool level, the thinly spread monies lost their effectiveness.[2]

Present preschool educational programs in New York City fall considerably short of universal coverage. Defining potential demand as the total 3-, 4-, and 5-year-old populations, current early childhood education covers only about 40 percent of this potential "market." Moreover, distribution of coverage that does exist is not always rational. A large number of 5-year-olds in poverty areas cannot be accommodated in kindergartens because of lack of space. In these same areas, however, prekindergarten classes are sometimes offered

[1] Fred M. Hechinger, ed., *Pre-school Education Today,* 1966.
[2] Dr. Deutsch has estimated that an effective preschool program costs between $1,000 and $1,200 per child a year. Expenses for kindergarten and prekindergarten in New York City public schools averaged $675 in 1967–68.

to disadvantaged 4-year-olds. These youngsters then take a year's "sabbatical" until they begin first grade.

For many welfare mothers who have dependent children, day care with the necessary quality educational component is sorely needed. In a survey of welfare families, about 60 percent of the mothers felt that they would prefer to work if adequate provision were made for their children.[1] Although additional funds for day care are available through federal and city agencies, planning and administrative delays have retarded necessary expansion of facilities. For example, the 1967 Social Security Amendments provide 75 percent in matching federal funds for day-care services to children of welfare recipients who are referred for work by the State Employment Service. However, only 10 percent of New York City welfare mothers have been referred. Professional day care, with a strong educational component for children of working mothers, costs about $1,800 per child per year. This is expensive, and efficient operation may well reduce this figure. However, on the other side of the balance are high welfare expenses and other costs associated with perpetuating the cycle of poverty and educational unpreparedness.

[1] Dr. Lawrence Podell, *Families on Welfare in New York City, 1969.*

Housing
in New York City

Of all the problems afflicting our urban areas, housing is the most visible. Perhaps more than any other single factor, housing establishes the quality of life. When housing is deteriorating or dilapidated, it spreads a darkening shadow across a city and its people. Poor housing breeds poverty, crime, and social chaos, depriving the young of even the hope of emerging from that environment. And conversely, good housing casts a whole new outlook across a city, providing new opportunities.

A housing shortage, unlike deficiencies in education or poverty or even transportation, cannot be corrected simply with imaginative programs. It will only respond to construction—the piling up of bricks and mortar. And that means large amounts of capital. With costs soaring, every resource must be recruited if the shortage is to be remedied. This implies a new form of public and private sector cooperation. Achieving that will entail as a first step broader understanding of the housing shortage as it exists today.

AN EMERGENT CONDITION Housing in New York City has reached a critical juncture. The free market mechanism for providing new units effectively has broken down. *The New York Times* reported in the fall of 1969, "Privately

financed apartment construction in the City is at one of the lowest levels in history. Outside of Manhattan, residential building activity is at a virtual standstill. During 1970, private apartment completions fell even more to a minuscule level of less than 2,800, a figure representing only 17 percent of the average for the 1950–1970 period." Government has not effectively stepped into the breach. The cumulative effects of neighborhood deterioration, abandonments, vandalism, and fire have caused recent losses of over 20,000 units per year, with another 10,000 lost annually through demolition.

New York City has about 2.9 million housing units, of which 75 percent represent rental housing. Seventy percent of this total, roughly 1,500,000 units, are over forty years old. Rising costs of maintenance, combined with poor restoration investment prospects, point clearly to the need for drastic reforms. Without them the city may become the slum capital of the country.

Both national and local forces have contributed to this situation. Nationally, especially prior to 1969, the lack of investment in housing contrasted sharply with the huge capital goods boom which carried into the late sixties. While other investment areas remained attractive, investment in housing lagged in the face of capital and labor shortages, inflation, rising interest, and tight money. The absence of a technologically rational housing industry fortified by an aggregate mass market and a guaranteed smooth flow of funds has added to the problem.

Locally, restrictive and costly zoning regulations, high-priced labor, land shortages reinforced by commercial competition for space, changing population composition, administrative red tape, and rent control have seriously complicated housing problems. These have not been improved by the sociological difficulties associated with large concentrations of poor people locked into the central city by discrimination and high home prices in the suburbs.

ORIGINS OF THE PROBLEM   During the sixties, in the face of a mere 1 percent growth in population, the number of housing units in New York City grew by 5 percent. Most of the latter occurred during the first half of the decade. Subsequently, new apartment construction fell drastically. Housing losses climbed, abandonments alone surpassing 90,000, contributing importantly to net losses in housing stock between 1966 and 1970.

While the inventory was increasing, the availability of additional units enabled a relatively steady population to divide itself into smaller households. Average household size declined sharply and the number of persons per rented apartment slipped by more than a fourth. The city's rate of rental vacancies dropped from 2.5 percent in 1960 to 2.0 percent in 1970, while homeowner vacancies in the same period fell from 1.1 to 0.7 percent.

Thus, the problem in New York City is not, as many have supposed, a simple matter of an insufficient number of dwelling units. What has happened is that a shortage has developed of clean, well-maintained apartments renting at reasonable prices in safe, livable neighborhoods. This condition can be attributed to deterioration and disinvestment brought about by neighborhood social breakdowns, to a lack of effective demand among the many low-income families, and to inadequate rental income flows attributable to rent control.

The core of New York City's housing problem rests on a seemingly intractable cost-income disparity. Increases in construction costs and mortgage and real estate tax rates make the private building of New York City apartment houses uneconomic except for the very high rent market. Unsatisfied housing needs bear most heavily on low- and moderate-income families, particularly those who have recently arrived in the city and who tend to be in minority groups. Lately, moreover, because of leaping costs, even middle-income families have found themselves priced out of the market for conventionally financed new housing.

In 1961, a new, conventionally financed two-bedroom apartment in a six-story elevator building would have rented for $210 a month, thus requiring an annual family income of close to $10,000. Today, such new apartments must rent at over $400 per month. With rent equivalent to 25 to 30 percent of income, the family must earn from $16,000 to $19,000 per year. Only about 7 percent of the city's households earn annual incomes of $15,000 and over.

RISING COSTS   In recent years new housing costs have risen considerably faster than the general price level, in the nation as well as in New York City. Building construction costs in New York City, as indicated by the *Engineering News-Record Index,* increased by 6.2 percent annually between 1966 and 1969, as compared with a 3.4 percent annual rise during the previous decade. This inflation in construction costs accelerated to over an 11 percent rate in the subsequent two years. Average room rents in newly planned, publicly assisted middle-income housing in New York City now are estimated between $70 and $90 per room per month, compared with $30 a decade ago.

ZONING A further contribution to high housing costs in New York City results from the zoning ordinance which became effective in December 1961. In addition to reducing the amount of land zoned for residential purposes, the new ordinance sharply reduced the amount of floor space a builder could erect on a given size plot. Sites became more difficult to assemble, and their costs rose because fewer could be economically developed and more time was required to obtain possession. In effect, the new zoning ordinance created an artificial land scarcity all over New York City.

Between 1962 and 1965 there was a temporary glut in New York's housing as private builders rushed completion of almost 100,000 apartments planned under the earlier, less restrictive zoning regulations. Predictably, apartment house construction dropped off sharply after this unusual surge.

RENT CONTROL Reflecting the growing imbalance between supply and demand occasioned by the drop in new construction and sharply rising costs of building and maintaining housing, apartment rents climbed in the late sixties, with particularly large jumps in 1968. These boosts were especially marked in the uncontrolled part of the city's inventory occupied by about one-third of the city's renter households. During 1968, median increases following two- or three-year leases were 26.5 percent and the median dollar increase per month per apartment was $45.40.[1] This situation led to enactment of a new city law limiting rent increases on renewals in two-thirds of the uncontrolled apartments to 10 percent on two-year leases and 15 percent on leases of three years. Increases for new tenants could be 15 percent on two-year and 25 percent on three-year leases. The very real threat that this limited extension of controls would be followed by the imposition of full rent regulation contributed further to the woes of New York's seriously ailing private housing industry.

Created to assure an adequate supply of moderate rent housing, New York City's old rent-control law shows evidence of having held rental income too low in relation to costs, and thus has been a contributing factor in many property owners' decisions to defer, if not neglect, maintenance. Owner abandonment of private residential properties has occurred on a uniquely huge scale in New York City during the past few years.

[1] *Report to the Mayor on an Investigation into Rental Increases in the Non-controlled Housing Market,* Housing and Development Administration, February 1969.

ADMINISTRATIVE INEFFICIENCIES

Lengthy bureaucratic delays and excessive red tape provide further examples of government-imposed hurdles to private housing development. Exasperating frustrations arise from the inconsistencies between public program goal rhetoric and the constraints imposed by the agencies responsible for the administration of those programs. Businessmen committed to ameliorating housing problems must stiffen their resolution in anticipation of burdensome impediments, because even the best of intentions and most unswerving dedication to the public good will not get them off the bureaucratic hook. For example, excessive delays in processing a project may eliminate a sponsor's profit allowance. Contractors doing business with the city must wait interminably for payment. Some add extra charges to compensate for this factor. Recently, a major developer complained bitterly about "rules, regulations and contract provisions which fly in the face of decades of custom and law in the construction industry, and force the contractor to pay legitimate construction costs out of his profit." Difficulties are not confined to local government. Governmental agencies find it difficult to carry out social objectives, such as creating more housing quickly, while at the same time having to pursue regulatory functions.

NEIGHBORHOOD DETERIORATION AND ABANDONMENT

Housing investment conditions are affected crucially by an entrepreneur's expectations of other investors' decisions in particular neighborhoods. Once under way, housing deterioration creates property-owner pessimism, the disinvestment becomes contagious, and the neighborhood breakdown occurs. This process stems from social as well as economic factors. Neighborhoods containing large quantities of old and obsolete residential buildings, where the middle class has moved out and poorer, disadvantaged groups have taken its place, illustrate the point. In these areas available housing has become occupied by lower-income tenants. Turnover has brought rents up to their economic level—in terms of tenant ability to pay. But the new residents' low income has kept vacancies high. This, in conjunction with already deteriorating housing, contributes to vandalism and eventual wholesale abandonments.

George Sternlieb, in *The Tenement Landlord,* demonstrates in his analysis of Newark slums that housing deterioration can take place even in the absence of rent controls. The ingredients of decay include changing population composition, a careless attitude toward property, a weakening of the market structure for rentals, disdain for rehabilitation, reduction in the scope and quality of municipal services, and

an appalling ignorance on the part of both landlords and tenants of the political and economic forces shaping their slums.

Abandonments aggravate the cancer of neighborhood breakdown. New York City has no central source that reports on abandoned buildings. Once a building is vacated, vandals quickly strip it of all removable equipment or materials that can bring a salvage price. The situation is worsened because property laws make city acquisition take up to four years to accomplish. In response to this problem it has been suggested that the state pass legislation to expedite city takeover of abandoned buildings.

COMMUNITY INVOLVEMENT

Problems arising from dealing with the people in the neighborhood of a proposed apartment building add to the socially related deterrents to housing investment. Securing the necessary community cooperation in building public or publicly assisted private housing—and more recently, even strictly private apartment construction—requires local involvement in all possible aspects of the development process, and is likely to impose difficult and tedious burdens of negotiation. Rarely is local leadership clearly identifiable. Too frequently, the struggle for power among community groups in disadvantaged areas prevents implementation of public assistance programs, including housing. When the Celanese Corporation of America and American Standard Incorporated formed a new corporation to produce housing in Harlem, factionalism within the community quickly became apparent. "One group believed that obtaining housing quickly was the most important consideration and Housing Authority ownership should be accepted if necessary. An opposing group maintained that community management of its housing was more important than time or even financial consideration."[1]

Albert A. Walsh, the city's Housing and Development Administrator, declared that he would not allow community groups in any neighborhood to veto any housing program, although he would consult with them closely on plans for new projects.[2]

The requirements that job opportunities arising from construction be given to lower-income persons residing in the area of such housing and that local businesses be awarded appropriate contracts for work impose added costs on some housing projects. From a social standpoint, however, these added costs could be more than offset by the enhanced skills, productivity, and earning power of local residents.

[1]Harold K. Bell and Granville H. Sewell, *Turnkey in New York, Evaluation of an Experiment,* School of Architecture, Columbia University, 1970.
[2]*New York Times,* Jan. 7, 1970, p. 47.

SCOPE AND EFFECTIVENESS   Public authorities at all levels of government have responded to housing needs by developing a proliferation of programs. By the end of 1970, public and publicly assisted private housing programs had contributed approximately 280,000 housing units, and these made up about 10 percent of New York City's inventory. In addition to the primary purpose of providing more and better shelter, public goals include the improvements of central city environments and bear the assumption that "new bricks" will uplift morale and improve social behavior. Aside from providing public housing for the poor, assistance includes technical and financial aid to nonprofit community-group sponsors, land-cost write-downs, tax abatements, and interest and rent subsidies, frequently in combination.

Combined public investment and operating costs resulted in a flow into the city's housing and renewal programs of $806 million during fiscal 1967–68.[1] Housing construction accounted for 88 percent of the $343 million capital spending, with most of the remainder devoted to land acquisition and clearance. Of the funds invested directly in housing ($315 million), 32 percent was channeled into low-income units, 45 percent served middle-income families, and 23 percent served families earning over $10,000 per year.

The record of the past few years demonstrates that bureaucratic redundancies, inefficiencies and delays, divided responsibilities, few appropriate locations, relocation and community-involvement difficulties, inadequate financing, and high and still-soaring development costs have seriously hindered public efforts. Governments have not been able to compensate for the elimination of an effective, profit-motivated private housing industry in New York City.

About the middle of 1969, federal housing programs ground to a halt in New York City because construction costs exceeded the statutory limitations built into the enabling legislation. Congress responded to this situation by raising the limitations from $3,150 to $4,200 per room. This enabled the reinstitution of federal programs here. Current costs, however, have again outstripped statutory limitations. Under 1972 cost conditions, it is necessary to combine both federal and state or local programs in order to bring rents down to the level of what low- and moderate-income families can pay.

The Housing and Urban Development Act of 1968 spurred housing production throughout the nation. But this has developed into a very costly operation. It is estimated that subsidized housing either started

[1]David Dreyfuss and John Hendrickson, *A Guide to Government Activities in New York City's Housing Markets,* The Rand Corporation, Santa Monica, California, 1968.

or projected for the three fiscal years 1970 through 1972 will obligate the federal government to subsidy payments of up to $30 billion over the next three or four decades. And assuming the completion of 6 million subsidized units, present estimates suggest there will be up to $7.5 billion required annually in subsidies by 1978.

Despite their cost and scale, federally and locally subsidized programs have not arrested the spread of neighborhood decline in older cities. In many instances, abandonments have exceeded the number of new or rehabilitated units built for low- and moderate-income families. Recently even government-sponsored projects have suffered from neighborhood deterioration, vandalism, and inefficient management. Soaring maintenance and operating costs, moreover, have put many projects in imminent danger of default because the income of tenants has not risen enough to permit the imposition of rents high enough to offset the increased costs of just running the projects, let alone paying off the capital investment.

Although there is a shortage of decent, reasonably priced accommodations in New York City, recently it has become difficult to fill some apartment houses built under the FHA "236" program. This comes about because regulations defining the income limits of the prospective tenants are so rigid that only a narrow band of New Yorkers can qualify for admission. Apartments, therefore, must remain empty or be filled by those receiving public assistance. As the Citizens Housing and Planning Council has pointed out, ". . . it is easier now to build for those who have no income, or relatively little income, than for those who while unable to find places in the unassisted private market, are nevertheless earning as much as twenty thousand dollars per year. . . ."

The present conglomeration of governmental housing programs, particularly federal subsidy programs, is confusing, inconsistent, and lacking in any meaningful coordination or set of priorities. The proposed Housing and Urban Development Act now before Congress contains provisions which will, it is hoped, correct some of these ills. For example, the bill places emphasis on preservation and improved management and maintenance of existing housing. A major new program would be initiated to help preserve older neighborhoods threatened by blight and abandonment. And the bill would expand the promising experimentation with housing allowances for low-income families.

PUBLIC-PRIVATE COOPERATION

Since governments have neither the resources nor the capabilities of building and managing large segments of the housing stock, they must place primary reliance on private industry. This awareness has led to greater emphasis on developing machinery for improved public-private cooperation. What began as a relatively narrow program designed to enable government to build housing for the poor has recently blossomed into a multifaceted approach. It seeks to combine the resources and expertise of private enterprise and government to create a relatively risk-free market for private investment in housing and urban renewal. In their efforts to improve the climate for attracting capital into residential construction, state and federal agencies offer comprehensive inducements. These include attempts to overcome antiquated and restrictive local building codes and zoning regulations, encouragement of technological innovations, and an earnest search for new sources of funds. Federal programs also place heavy reliance on tax incentives.

The United States Housing and Urban Development Act of 1968 (Act of 1968) and New York State's Limited Profit Companies law (Mitchell-Lama) provide the principal legislative bases for encouraging private organizations to invest in low- and moderate-income housing and realize competitive yields.

An important facet of the Act of 1968 authorizes national banks to participate in the creation and operation of federally chartered, privately funded corporations which would mobilize private investment and business skills in producing low- and moderate-income housing in volume. Tax advantages would be used as lures. The parent corporation, the National Corporation for Housing Partnerships, would form a local partnership as its vehicle for participating in local housing developments, pursuant to federal and local programs. The parent organization would contribute part of the seed money or initial expenditures of the local partnership. This system reduces the risk of loss which might occur on any one project by permitting industrial and financing firms to pool their investments and spread their risks over a number of projects.

MAKING HOUSING INVESTMENT ATTRACTIVE

Housing-assistance legislation permits investors in low- and moderate-income housing to gain financial rewards in several ways. Primarily, these include development fees and various forms of tax benefits. For example, the interest subsidies provided by the Act of 1968 to reduce rents or carrying charges may add significantly to a sponsor's yield. The same federal legislation encourages private developers by

permitting the Department of Housing and Urban Development (HUD) to finance 100 percent of a project's purchase price when the sponsor (builder-investor) wishes to sell the project to a nonprofit corporation or cooperative composed of the project's tenants. In such a case, the sale price could be sufficient to permit the builder-investor to recover his full costs, equity investment, and sufficient cash to pay the taxes due on the sale.

Housing developments require sponsors who furnish management skills as well as seed money to get a project started. Such sponsors may capitalize their entrepreneurial effort and thus enhance their returns. A 10 percent "sponsor-builder's risk allowance" may be added to the costs of a project (exclusive of land) for determining the amount of a private HUD-insured mortgage. This allowance is provided for a developer who is a member of the sponsor partnership and who actually plans the land assembly, financing, building, and operation of a project. A similar arrangement exists under New York State and New York City Mitchell-Lama projects, except that the sponsor's fee percentage is less than in the case of HUD and diminishes as project values rise.

Federal tax incentives make it possible for sponsors to realize an attractive rate of return on housing by reducing their tax on other incomes (tax shelters). It is important to emphasize that the sponsor may depreciate the entire cost of a building, even though 90 percent is paid with borrowed funds for which the sponsor has no personal liability. The depreciable amount permitted includes the carrying charges previously deducted during construction.

Housing investors generally use an accelerated method of depreciation. This method results in larger paper tax losses in the early years of a project. Tax losses, and therefore tax savings, are further enhanced in the early years because of the technique of computing mortgage payments. HUD and Mitchell-Lama mortgages generally require level payments (including both interest and principal). The early payments, therefore, consist primarily of interest which is deductible for tax purposes.

SOME CAVEATS Governmental resources, beset by many conflicting demands, set definite limits on the funds that can be devoted to housing. Rising construction and operation costs, necessarily limited appropriations, statutory cost ceilings, and family income restrictions, even if made more generous, will continue to make housing production most difficult to achieve, especially in high-cost areas such as New York City.

Industry's greatest housing challenge lies in exploiting its problem-solving capacities and presumed efficiencies in the development of housing for low- and moderate-income families, utilizing all available public aid, but within the constraints cited above.

GOOD HOUSING COULD BE GOOD BUSINESS

Private industry has an important self-interest in the creation of more and better housing in New York City and in the continued viability of its environment. New York is the business headquarters of the nation and shows every sign of remaining so despite forecasts to the contrary. Housing activities designed to combat ghetto blight and improve the stock of dwellings, in conjunction with parallel efforts in employment, education, and economic development, will help materially in sustaining a strong city. Furthermore, demographic and economic trends indicate that the inner-city minority group populations constitute potential markets of rapidly growing proportions. They will constitute increasingly large shares of the city's labor force. Rising standards have tended to persuade workers at all levels that they require adequate housing associated with pleasant and interesting amenities. The difficulties in the local market increasingly require that housing no longer be taken for granted but must actively be provided by establishments wishing to attract and keep qualified personnel. Helping satisfy housing needs, therefore, means more than just performing good deeds.

The huge dimensions of New York's largely unpenetrated housing market present enormous opportunities as well as challenges. Estimates of New York's total housing needs in the next decade vary from 50,000 to 60,000 new and rehabilitated units a year. The latter figure is more realistic, to wit:

1. Some 10,000 new units annually to accommodate new households and further reduce overcrowding.
2. An estimated 20,000 new units a year to replace substandard and abandoned "old law" tenements built before 1901.
3. Another 30,000 a year in partial or substantial rehabilitation to arrest the deterioration of about half of the "new law" tenements built before 1929.

IMPROVING THE INVESTMENT CLIMATE

Before they train their weapons on the target of mass housing production, in New York City or elsewhere, owners and managers of large financial and industrial corporations must first be convinced of the political feasibility as well as the potential economic and social bene-

fits. Governments must create a radically improved climate for such commitment. This means appropriate monetary outlays, firm and unambiguous cooperation with housing entrepreneurs, and drastic reform of administrative agencies so that they help, rather than hinder, project development. The conventional practice of consuming years in redundant paperwork and endless negotiations must give way to a less cumbersome procedure. The huge investment required in city rebuilding implies no small act of faith on the part of both builder and government.

One other way for local government to contribute significantly to an improved climate for urban renewal is to act as a buffer between community groups and the developer. Neighborhood citizen involvement is fully justified. In fact, no plan is workable without its contribution. Businesses engaged in housing affairs should expect and seek as much community involvement as feasible. They cannot, however, be expected to sustain their investments in costly and excessively protracted conflicts with local factions.

In view of the deterrent to investment imposed by New York City's rent control system, it appears necessary to amend controls gradually and reactivate free market conditions. The vacancy decontrol law passed by New York State in 1971 is a step in the right direction. Suggested changes would permit fair market rents, which would improve rental income enough to provide for an adequate return on investment and encourage proper operation and maintenance of structures. In exchange for permitting more flexible rents, the city could require the allocation of some of this added income to improved maintenance and would conduct strict code-enforcement inspections. Where rents rise beyond the ability of various tenants to pay, public subsidies might make up the difference between what the tenants could afford and the economic rent of an apartment.

FIX UP OR REPLACE   The most rapid means of increasing the stock of decent housing would seem to lie in large-scale rehabilitation of sound buildings. The existence within New York City of many thousands of such structures which have slipped into deterioration (or will soon do so) clearly points to an approach which would compensate for deferred maintenance and revitalize old neighborhoods. In view of the immense difficulties of replacement, it obviously makes more sense to preserve and use existing reclaimable stock rather than to let it go down the drain. Rehabilitation also reduces the problems of relocation and community upheaval that the bulldozer approach to urban renewal usually brings.

A large enough scale of rehabilitation might encourage a new modernization industry for builders and suppliers, with consequent economies of scale as well as increased employment and business opportunities for residents of the neighborhoods affected. This can be of particular significance in disadvantaged areas. The process, moreover, might give rise to technological advances such as the development of new products and systems which could also be of value in other aspects of the building industry.

Despite these apparent advantages, rehabilitation has not produced a significant number of improved housing units in New York City. Experience under the city's Municipal Loan Program, for example, has indicated that the cost of revamped dwellings suffers in comparison with that of new apartments produced under the Mitchell-Lama program. This is largely due to the fact that most structures reworked thus far have tended to be scattered old four- or five-story walk-ups where unforeseeable complexities imposed high repair costs and the finished product still provided an obsolete layout. Rehabilitation is probably least feasible in the case of those buildings which require practically complete reconstruction. But there are substantial advantages in rehabilitation applied on a major scale to sound post-World War I structures, where replacement of bathroom and kitchen facilities and possibly new roofs and heating systems constitute the principal needed repairs. In order for rehabilitation to exercise maximum impact on neighborhood improvement, the buildings should be geographically concentrated rather than isolated.

Large areas of the city stand on the brink of deteriorating into slums. Blocks of properties are ripe for acquisition and assembly. A dedicated management group could develop the technical apparatus for their rehabilitation. Concurrently, there should be broad experimentation with community participation, tenant-owner cooperatives, local labor and business involvement in the actual reconstruction work, job and management training, and the structuring of indigenous operation and maintenance organizations. Housing can be preserved and neighborhoods revitalized under such conditions, provided municipal authorities cooperate by improving city services in the area.

TURNKEY A relatively new and rapid method by which a private developer can contribute to the low-income housing stock is to construct a building and sell it, along with the land, to a local housing authority for use as public housing. This "turnkey" approach automatically avoids a great deal of bureaucratic red tape.

Turnkey was off to a slow start in New York where it faced the legal obstacle of the Wicks law, which requires that any contracts by a housing authority for work exceeding $25,000 must have separate bidding and contracting for plumbing, heating, and electrical installations. New York State attorneys maintained that any construction agreement concerning public housing must conform to the law. Federal authorities, on the other hand, insisted that a turnkey contract is for a completed building, not for the actual construction, and that the Wicks law was not applicable.

The authorities found a way out of this dilemma by invoking a surprisingly effective gentlemen's agreement with public-spirited developers. When the American Standard Corporation and the Celanese Corporation formed "Construction for Progress, Incorporated" to construct housing in Harlem, their only basis for expecting the Housing Authority to purchase the completed building was a "handshake" acquisition agreement. A similar arrangement took place between the Housing Authority and a development corporation created by the New York Bank for Savings and the Bowery Savings Bank. In cooperation with the Upper Park Avenue Community Association, these banks have built two apartment houses in Harlem.

Over the past year, however, the legal tangles were resolved and conventional contracts are now being signed between developers and the Housing Authority in accordance with a prescribed HUD formula. Twenty-six new projects were contracted for in 1971, and by removing the risks to builders implicit in "handshake" agreements, new projects should continue to be undertaken at a faster rate. The growing pressure for more low-rent public housing in New York City will likely bring about more intensive use of the turnkey device.

OTHER INNOVATIONS Analysts often have attributed the relatively high cost of homes and the apparently slow gains in housing productivity largely to fragmentation in the industry. In the United States the average homebuilder's operations are limited to fewer than twenty-five dwelling units per year. The typical home-construction operation precludes mass-production techniques and the use of experimental or new methods and materials.

Soaring construction costs have prompted both the federal government and New York State to institute programs to encourage new construction concepts, products, systems, and procedures. Under federal auspices Operation Breakthrough, administered by HUD, seeks to promote government-business partnerships which will combine new methods with the creation of a mass market through subsidies and, it is hoped, a large volume of housing. In a similar vein, Governor Rockefeller, seeking "to create a receptive climate for industry to provide the technological innovations that can reduce housing costs," charged the state's Urban Development Corporation to launch a "new effort in public/private cooperation."

From a technical standpoint, two innovations seem especially promising in promoting productivity in housing. One involves the use of reinforced concrete in high-rise construction. The seventy-story Lake Towers apartment building in Chicago exemplifies the possibilities. Some American firms have acquired rights for the use of foreign techniques, where the standard practice is to pour concrete modules and slabs at the building site.

Factory manufacture of module units which can be assembled on a production line, with plumbing and electrical work performed as subassemblies, represents a new industry of explosive potential. The high probability of continuing improvements in the new production systems raises the possibility that productivity gains may offset rising materials prices. Module houses, conventional in every respect except for method of assembly, can be turned out in far less time and cost than homes constructed in the traditional way. Most important, however, is the potential for volume construction.

The module principle of apartment construction, possibly utilizing a system of stacked concrete units, provides an important promise of applicability in New York City. Appliances, electrical and plumbing fittings, even furniture and carpets, can be put in place in the unit on the ground, in a covered, weatherproof shed, at the job site, utilizing conventional building-trades skills. Such units are then lifted into place, and can be arranged in a variety of architectural styles, with great facade design flexibility. The estimated cost savings resulting from an "all-weather" system may reach as high as 15 to 18 percent over conventional apartment construction techniques. Utilization of construction trade-union labor may help get the technique accepted in New York City.

The scarcity of capital for investment in housing has given rise to several suggested innovations in this area too. One involves the use of "special assistance funds" in a "tandem plan." The plan authorizes the Government National Mortgage Association (GNMA) to make mortgage commitments to nonprofit sponsors of rental and cooperative housing under Section 236 of the Act of 1968 with the Federal National Mortgage Association (FNMA) agreeing to take

over the long-term mortgages from GNMA for less than GNMA paid for them.

The National Corporation for Housing Partnerships filed a registration statement with the Securities and Exchange Commission to raise $50 million for seed money. By the spring of 1972, Housing Partnerships had received payment of $13.1 million from its investors representing 270 lending corporations, utilities, banks, insurance companies, and labor unions. A balance of $42.1 million subscription is on call when needed.

An additional potential incentive for housing production exists in the proposed Community Credit Expansion Bill, introduced in 1969 by Senator William Proxmire of Wisconsin. Under the bill, either existing financial institutions or newly created special institutions, to be known as National Development Banks, would be provided with substantial subsidies and guarantees in order to make loans for housing in low-income areas.

CITIBUILDING Our large-scale housing needs and the existence of a potential mass market are obvious. Assuming government commitment of a smooth flow of funds on a long-term basis, home-development consortia combining the talents of large financial and industrial organizations could deal effectively with the housing supply problem. Well-capitalized consortia can deploy management skills in depth. They can buy land or materials in large quantities and at lower prices than the small operator. The large development company can partially offset increases in costs of labor and materials by higher productivity— through intensive use of factory-assembled standardized components. It can institute computer-programmed cost controls. The consortium's access to financing is a major advantage. It can meet capital requirements via the public market as well as through other traditional sources at lower cost than ordinary construction loans. By engaging in operations in more than one area, a major consortium can spread its risk and offset low profits in one project by greater success in another. Most importantly, such organizations can apply the sophistication and exploit the resources necessary for the comprehensive planning and redevelopment of entire neighborhoods. The goals of the consortium would be to produce the largest volume of quality housing at the least cost by integrating management, market, land, capital, planning, design, and long-term financing in a systems-oriented approach.

This does not mean marshaling huge efforts for the single-dimensional purpose of producing housing on a crash basis. Too often, programs have been implemented without taking into account their long-range impacts. Urban systems, up to now, have represented largely the abstractions of analysts who have attempted to rationalize diverse and frequently incompatible forms of development. The systems approach makes essential an awareness of the consequences of development programs—consequences which must be anticipated and compensated for on a firmer base than intuitive judgment. The numerous interrelationships between housing and its environment and the effects of changing key economic and social variables available to decision makers must be understood. Great care must be taken to prevent action that will make the situation worse.

The potential of this approach is substantial. But so are the problems of such large-scale "human engineering." Goals must be realistic and attainable and the housing must be appropriate to income levels, size of family, and other social characteristics. Where to build? If slums are demolished and new housing put in place in the same area, will it not be self-defeating to encourage immigration into an improved center city while available and appropriate employment is found increasingly in relatively inaccessible suburban places? If housing for the poor can be built only where the poor live, whatever their color, then it may be physically impossible to meet the growing goals for appropriate housing.

The problem of working with rather than against market forces to achieve optimal land use raises the question of the advisability of placing homes on expensive central city land where residences must compete with commercial demands for space. A satisfactory answer to this question must embrace a careful evaluation of the future role of the central city. Technological developments which emphasize communications and expanded opportunities for exchange of goods and ideas, and which have brought about the huge concentrations of central management and white-collar workers, would suggest that the residences be placed elsewhere than in the city core. It would seem more logical to increase population densities in the outer reaches of the city (e.g., waterfront properties currently owned, but no longer required, by the military) or in "inner ring" suburban areas (under extraterritorial leasing arrangements if necessary), freeing the core to perform its essentially commercial function.

. . . AND BUILDING A BETTER CITY   Even well-conceived, large-scale "citibuilding" and rehabilitation projects are not the ultimate key to solving New York's housing crisis.

For, in the final analysis, inadequate housing is only a symptom of much deeper problems. People will live in adequate housing only when they have sufficient money to pay for it.

In the short run, public subsidies—either outright or in the form of interest subsidization or rent supplements—can help the poor find decent housing. For the long run, however, means will have to be found to enable the poor to raise their incomes so that they can bid freely in the housing market.

The way to ensure better housing for the poor is not simply to build and rehabilitate homes, but, more fundamentally, to expand job opportunities and improve the capabilities of the disadvantaged through education and training. To be sure, much employment can originate from a massive housing program itself. New commercial and industrial facilities created as part of the "citibuilding" process will generate even more jobs.

In short, housing policy, instead of being oriented toward constraints (e.g., rent control), must become part of a broader thrust to expand human opportunities. Any successful approach to housing will have to be integrated with policies to promote education and develop human resources, economic growth, and well-being. Through large-scale development and redevelopment of all our resources, a coordinated, comprehensive program can help forge a new economic frontier from the raw material of underutilized or improperly utilized manpower, public programs, and private initiative, in the context of the vast opportunities of this great city.

The Transportation Problem

No rapid-transit system covers as much ground, carries as many passengers, costs as much to operate, or fills a comparable role in a community as New York's subway system. A vital link in the city's life, it is the keystone in a network of public and private transportational modes that moves hundreds of thousands of people in predictable tides at the start and end of each day. The system, huge and sprawling as it is, actually is delicately balanced. When its interrelated parts slip out of phase, even a localized service interruption can create rippling effects, creating widespread delays for thousands of people. Such events, while they emphasize to riders the deficiencies of the system, impress them equally with the absolute necessity for the mass-transit services.

A careful look at an urban center's transportation system makes the complexity of urban life plain. A reliable mode of transport figures in such personal decisions as where to work, what kind of work to do, and where to live. The relationship between transport and everyday life makes the system a highly personal service despite its universality. Like the air around us, it is available to all and essential to most.

The principal transportation task confronting the New York metropolitan area is to get more than 2 million people to and from work

And Now, the Sever

New York Pos

Mayor on LIRR Loa...

HOW ABOUT TH
SUBWAY FARE

Sterility Warning on Pill

in Manhattan's central business district below 60th Street from all parts of the region via an efficient and high-quality mass-transit system. Fulfilling this daily task requires accommodation to a tremendous volume of movement under extremely difficult space limitations. This is a formidable accomplishment when everything works smoothly, but a rich source of irritation and complaint when any major part of the system breaks down.

Although only mass transit can meet the journey-to-work requirements, it has not succeeded in overcoming the congestion and obstacles to personal mobility created by the center city's huge concentration of jobs and people. This problem is neither unique to New York nor new. In 1905, congested traffic at rush hours was described as "the number one problem of large cities in the United States, and pictures of urban traffic jams in the days of horse-drawn vehicles and electric cars attest to the fact that congestion was bad long before the motor vehicles made it worse."[1]

Currently, 9 square miles of Manhattan daily ingest a huge work force of over 2 million persons, a number larger than the combined population of Baltimore, Boston, and Cincinnati. The New York City "commutershed," with a population of about 18 million, extends to places as distant as Trenton, Poughkeepsie, New Haven, and Riverhead and embraces 8,000 square miles in 3 states, 25 counties, and approximately 1,400 political jurisdictions. Of the workers entering the central business district, each business day, about 667,000 are Manhattan residents, approximately 1 million come from the rest of New York City, and some 380,000 from the suburban communities. Long Island's Nassau and Suffolk Counties account for some 130,000, and 84,000 come in from Westchester County and Connecticut. The remainder travel from west of the Hudson, primarily New Jersey.

The private automobile does not play a paramount role in transporting people to Manhattan, since mass transit brings in over 82 percent of all central-business-district workers. About two-thirds arrive during the rush hour alone. Commuter railroads, and to a lesser extent, express buses, have the task of delivering the outer residents to Manhattan. The urban mass-transit system, consisting of the subways and supported by buses, handles the shorter journeys within the dense core of the region. The subway system, by far the dominant transit mode, delivers over 1 million people into the central business district each workday morning.

[1] Wilfred Owen, *The Metropolitan Transportation Problem*, The Brookings Institution, Washington, D.C. p. 6.

Despite their essential function, however, mass-transit facilities have been allowed to decay. The relatively recent intervention of the federal government, as well as of the states of New York, New Jersey, and Connecticut, into the public transportation field has only begun to offset the service and equipment deterioration that has been occurring over more than a generation in this region. Thousands of suburban commuters still must board obsolete and undependable rolling stock whose state of dilapidation starkly reflects long years of neglect. New York City has expended approximately $2 billion since World War II in attempting to modernize its subway system. Even this large sum has proven inadequate to rehabilitate a system in which the IRT lines were substantially completed in the early 1900s, the BMT lines in the 1920s, and the IND lines ten years later. Thus, a residue of worn-out and sometimes ill-maintained equipment frequently imposes on city residents some of the most uncomfortable and uncertain aspects of their workday routines.

ECONOMIC INPUT In addition to the personal hardships imposed, the costs associated with lateness at times have assumed serious proportions. For example, during the transit strike of 1966, absenteeism, especially prevalent during the early days of the strike, caused a loss of about $2\frac{1}{2}$ million man-days. Reduced hours for workers present during only part of the day created an even more drastic time loss. More recently, the subway and suburban railroad service breakdowns during the very cold weather of early 1970 created a near-emergency situation for Manhattan-bound commuters as well as for their employers; 22 percent of subway trains were "behind schedule." Since then, the New York City Transit Authority has augmented significantly its maintenance personnel. The situation improved to the point where during 1970 average on-time performance rose to 83 percent. This improvement continued during 1971.

Regional transit difficulties, moreover, seriously impair the ability of establishments in the central business district to recruit qualified personnel. The condition applies particularly to the younger persons of promise who shy away from employment in New York because of urban problems such as transportation. One of the most important advantages of a central-business-district location is the potential supply of employees with varieties of skills and qualifications. To the extent that transportation deficiencies impose handicaps on employee availability, they vitiate an essential element of the city's economic life.

THE DAILY FLOW OF WORKERS INTO MANHATTAN SOUTH OF 59TH STREET
(in thousands of work trips)

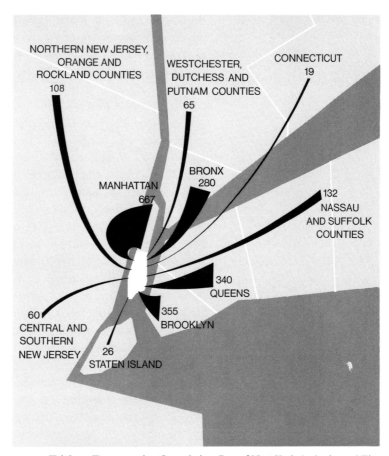

NORTHERN NEW JERSEY, ORANGE AND ROCKLAND COUNTIES
108

WESTCHESTER, DUTCHESS AND PUTNAM COUNTIES
65

CONNECTICUT
19

BRONX
280

MANHATTAN
667

132
NASSAU AND SUFFOLK COUNTIES

340
QUEENS

355
BROOKLYN

60
CENTRAL AND SOUTHERN NEW JERSEY

26
STATEN ISLAND

SOURCE: Tri-State Transportation Commission, Port of New York Authority and First National City Bank estimate.

CIRCULATION

After reaching their destinations in the central business district, commuters face serious crowding problems. These begin with the station platforms and walkways and end at an office or other work site. Conventionally, this kind of short-distance transportation has been achieved by buses or taxicabs or by walking. Growing congestion, particularly in such areas as east midtown and the downtown financial district, has made the trip from station to office more difficult. At times midday traffic, both pedestrian and vehicular, achieves virtual paralysis in some areas of the city. For example, the combination of narrow streets and very large numbers of people, mixed with widespread illegal parking practices, made the lower Manhattan area so congested as to require the imposition of the strictest no-parking rules of any area of the city on September 23, 1970.

135   Transportation

An efficient, well-run transportation system can contribute greatly to the smooth functioning of business and to life in general in a major metropolitan area such as New York. The corollary is equally true, if more painful: an inefficient transportation system speeds the deterioration of the quality of life in an urban environment. Instead of benefiting from anticipated transportation improvements due to presumed technical advances, commuters have found it barely possible to maintain older travel-time schedules in their work journeys. It is not surprising, therefore, that people impatiently demand to know why New York's public transportation system does not work better. More pointedly, they are asking how and when it can be put right.

Technicians know, of course, what a transportation system can reasonably be expected to do. Their efforts are directed not only to making the system work, but also to performing in accordance with standards appropriate to a highly interdependent regional community. Techniques, however, cannot by themselves transform the existing piecemeal collection of transportation facilities into a workable regional system of sustained quality. Achieving improved and coordinated transportation will require, in addition to the allocation of far greater public resources than have been provided in the past, the achievement of a consensus in the region and the support of all concerned groups. People must be willing to pay the bill, not only for capital investments but also for operational deficits. Meeting such costs (and creating appropriate operational supervisory safeguards) may be substantially less burdensome, however, than the diseconomies generated by transportation systems which are inadequately funded to meet the region's needs.

THE REGION'S MASS TRANSIT FACILITIES

THE SUBWAY SYSTEM

The New York City subway-elevated system, an $8 billion property owned by the municipal government but operated by a state agency, the New York City Transit Authority, employs about 43,000 people and transports an average of 4.2 million riders daily in almost 7,000 cars on approximately 240 route miles of track. Although London's rapid-transit system in terms of track mileage is almost as long, New York is surpassed in terms of passengers carried only by Moscow where 1.5 billion passengers were carried in 1969 (compared to 1.2 billion in New York.)

Operating expenses of the New York City subways amounted to $403 million in fiscal 1970. Debt service charges paid by the city

approximated $144 million, and the city's bill for the transit police stood at $58 million. Total operating costs thus surpassed $600 million. During fiscal 1971, operating expenses rose to $482 million, and the level for the year ending June 30, 1972, without taking account of a new wage contract for the transit workers, will be substantially higher. With regard to capital investment, the city has borne the lion's share. Federal contributions thus far have been minor, and the state's inputs are just beginning.

Practically all subway revenues come from passenger fares. City payments to the Transit Authority for transporting school children and the aged at reduced fares amounted to $37 million in fiscal 1970. Other income results from advertising and concession rentals. Despite the increase in fares in January 1970 to 30 cents and the injection into operating funds of $26 million in surplus revenues from the Triborough Bridge and Tunnel Authority,[1] the subway system incurred an operating deficit of almost $64 million during the fiscal year ending June 30, 1970. The deficit for fiscal 1971 neared $100 million, and the disparity between costs and revenues during the fiscal year ending June 30, 1972 rose even more to a level of $133 million. This happened despite the January 1972 fare increase from 30 to 35 cents.

Mass-transit fares traditionally have been kept as low as possible whether the system was run by private industry, the city, or the Transit Authority. This policy has limited the growth of revenues but has not kept costs from rising. Required by statute to cover operating expenses mainly from the fare box (plus whatever sums the city would contribute voluntarily), and faced with growing, huge deficits, the Transit Authority has been under inexorable pressure to raise fares. Such a move, however, depending on its size, could exert a strong handicap on the city's economy and would further diminish patronage. New York's rapid-transit industry is caught in an all-too-familiar vicious circle. Constantly growing costs and a long-term decline in patronage have been accompanied by poorer service and rising fares, which, in turn, have brought about a further drop in the number of passengers.

[1] The New York City Transit Authority actually received $74 million of these funds on July 1, 1970. The total included $26 million surplus from 1969 in addition to revenues left over from the previous two years. In return, New York City had to pledge, in 1968, $100 million a year for five years for capital investment in the subway system for projects requested by the Transit Authority.

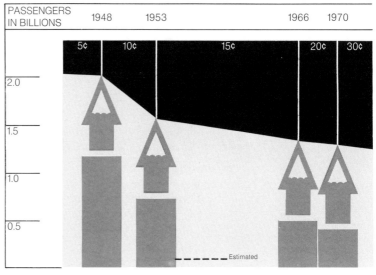

SOURCE: New York City Transit Authority.

The 50 percent increase in fares in January 1970 was followed by a 5 percent reduction in traffic (see chart).[1] It also generated intense indignation among the city's riders, who found the incongruity between high fares and deteriorating service a little too much to bear.

The situation had been aggravated by curtailed maintenance practices. These resulted from inadequate revenues and were geared to illusory short-term economies aimed more at holding fares down than at upkeep and the efficient operation of equipment. Between 1953 and 1966, for example, the work force had been reduced by about 6,000 employees in efforts to hold down the fare. In 1953 the Transit Authority employed 2,100 more skilled mechanics than the 7,239 on the 1969 roster, according to data cited in a Transport Workers Union advertisement in *The New York Times* on September 17, 1970. The Transit Authority asserts that employee paring was made possible through mechanization of maintenance procedures.

Another obstacle to effective maintenance of the city's subway system arose inadvertently as a result of the introduction of more generous retirement benefits. Between July 1, 1968, and the end of 1970 the Transit Authority lost approximately 7,000 of its best-trained maintenance and operating personnel.

A vigorous recruitment program to compensate for this anticipated

[1] January through June 1970 compared to the same period in 1969.

exodus did not begin until January 1970. According to Transit Authority spokesmen, the primary reason for this turnabout was the availability of funds, attributable to the 10-cent rise in fares. In addition, the Transit Authority had reached an agreement with the city whereby it could cut the red tape in hiring rather than go through the time-consuming conventional civil service routine. Simultaneously, cutbacks in defense spending and the slowdown in the economy threw thousands of relatively experienced men into the job market. The same generous employment provisions which led to so many retirements also attracted many men. Their availability has given the Transity Authority an opportunity to implement new inspection, overhauling, cleaning, and painting schedules.

New overhauling procedures were badly needed. In a special study, a panel of experts declared that "maintenance programs have not been adhered to in recent years; that there have been significant differences between the standards of inspection in different service shops; and that regular workshop overhaul of cars, having been virtually at a standstill for some years, was effectively restored only in 1968."[1] The panel's report went on to say, "In the present situation, with a large backlog of cars overdue for workshop overhaul, 550 cars a year are programmed for overhaul. At this rate, it will be 1975 before the 12-year or 600,000-mile overhaul interval has been achieved throughout the fleet." The panel asserted that such a schedule would prove unsatisfactory and would contribute to "service failures at the high levels of recent years. . . ."

In its 1971 Annual Report, the Metropolitan Transportation Authority declared that the number of complete car overhauls reached 530. This represented a significant increase over the 332 completed the year before.[2]

In 1969, the city introduced air-conditioned subway cars. At the present time, about 700 such cars are in operation, and by 1975 about

[1] Report of the Panel Appointed to Study the Safety of Train Operations on the Subway System of the New York Transit Authority, Nov. 13, 1970.

[2] The Metropolitan Transportation Authority is a public authority chartered by New York State in 1968. It is authorized to provide policy direction and control for several existing transportation agencies (Transit Authority, Long Island Railroad, Triborough Bridge and Tunnel Authority, Manhattan and Bronx Surface Transit Operating Authority, Staten Island Rapid Transit Operating Authority) in the area that includes New York City and Nassau, Suffolk, Westchester, Putnam, Dutchess, Rockland, and Orange Counties. Each constituent agency, under the common policy direction of the Metropolitan Transportation Authority Board and its chairman serving as chief executive officer, is responsible for its own operations and management. Each working day about 8.5 million people use the MTA's subway, bus, rail, air, and bridge and tunnel services; they are served by some 58,000 employees.

one-fourth of the system's fleet will be air-conditioned. This will include half of the BMT-IND division. The IRT lines were refurbished with new cars before the air-conditioning program began. Space considerations, moreover, preclude installation on IRT cars of the kind of cooling equipment put into cars on the other lines. Efforts to air-condition the newer IRT cars are underway, with contracts let to two companies to design workable equipment. The Transit Authority also has designed and the city has ordered 352 new 75-foot cars, 8 of which can carry the load of 10 of the older version. The city and MTA have requested a grant from the federal government to permit purchase of 750 additional similar cars.

The shift of the city's population away from the central areas well served by rapid transit has created a serious mismatch between available rapid-transit services and the areas of greatest need. In response to these service deficiencies, the Metropolitan Transportation Authority has planned an expansion of the subway system, estimated in 1969 to cost some $1.4 billion. But the program will probably require at least ten years for completion, and there is every likelihood that inflation will boost the final bill to $2.5 billion or more. The state has fixed its contribution at $600 million, leaving an approximate $2 billion burden on New York City's capital budget. Whether the anticipated level of federal contributions will diminish substantially the city's financial load depends upon action taken by the Congress on current mass-transit-aid bills.

On the basis of plans associated with the passage of the New York State 1967 Transportation Bond Issue, the MTA published details of a subway expansion program. Designed to reach outer areas now poorly served by rapid transit and to relieve overcrowding on such lines as the Lexington Avenue and the Queens Boulevard, the planned subway expansion features a new Second Avenue subway, extending from the East Bronx to lower Manhattan. Construction should begin in the fall of 1972 on the portion north of 34th Street. A tunnel under the East River at 63rd Street in Manhattan, which will serve both subways and the Long Island Railroad, is nearly completed. Construction has also begun on an interconnection between the Queens lines and the Second Avenue, Sixth Avenue, and BMT lines at 63rd Street in Manhattan.

To serve northeast Queens, a two-track line will extend from the Queens Boulevard subway in the Elmhurst area following the Long Island Expressway to Kissena Boulevard. A southeast Queens line will extend from the Queens Boulevard line at Van Wyck Expressway

along the Atlantic branch of the Long Island Railroad to Springfield Gardens. Another Queens rapid-transit improvement will be a "super-express" bypass along the Long Island Railroad's main line from Forest Hills to Queens Plaza. In Manhattan, a lower East Side loop running along Avenue C will link the sixth Avenue IND with the 14th Street Canarsie line and serve an area distant from existing subways. In Brooklyn, the Nostrand Avenue line will be extended from Avenue H to Avenue W and the Utica Avenue line from Eastern Parkway to Avenue U. There is also a plan, fallen in priority because of inadequate funds, to improve central-business-district transportation with a transit line or other type of "people mover" across 48th Street. In view of the sharp rises in costs since the formulation of the expansion program, and also because of the defeat of the 1971 Transportation Bond Issue, the question has arisen concerning how much construction the present level of available funds will permit. Nevertheless, key construction programs, such as the Second Avenue subway and the 63rd Street tunnel, continue to progress.

In any case, the Transit Authority and the Metropolitan Transportation Authority have completed the necessary planning and preliminary engineering. All these programs, representing the first substantial subway extensions in thirty years, have secured the approval of New York City's Board of Estimate. Despite their large scale, however, it is expected that the new routes will improve the quality of service to present users rather than generate any significant number of new rapid-transit commuters. "Crowding and travel time will be reduced, but the bulk of the operating costs of the new lines will not be covered by revenues received from new passengers."[1] Expansion of the subway system by about 20 percent to 290 route miles will add considerably to debt service as well.

The added facilities, when fully operative (and at 1970 prices), will incur an estimated $175 million a year in operating expenses and $245 million a year in debt service and amortization, bringing the total cost to $420 million. A 5 percent increase in patronage, as anticipated by the Metropolitan Transportation Authority, would accrue over $20 million a year in offsetting revenues at the 35-cent fare level. Some revenue will be lost, however, as a consequence of the reduced need for many riders to pay both bus and subway fares.

From July 1946 until June 1953, when the Transit Authority as-

[1] *Standards for Rapid Transit Expansion—A Report to the Mayor and the New York City Board of Estimate,* Transportation Administration, City Planning Commission, Bureau of the Budget, August 1968, p. 8.

sumed operating responsibility, the city subsidized transit operations directly in the amount of $108 million. Since then, the system has operated in the red during thirteen of the nineteen years of Transit Authority responsibility. The significant potential increases in the rapid-transit system's debt service and operating expenses make all the more critical the need to develop a fiscal policy adequate to cope with constantly rising costs and recurrent deficits. It is increasingly urgent, therefore, to structure an equitable arrangement for the distribution of costs between users and the public, to broaden rapid transit's revenue base, and to pursue vigorously all cost savings consistent with efficient operation.

COMMUTER RAILROADS The suburban railroads in the New York metropolitan area include the Long Island Railroad and the New Haven, Hudson, and Harlem divisions of the Penn Central, all serving commuters east of the Hudson. The Penn Central line entering Manhattan at West 32nd Street, the Central Railroad of New Jersey, and the Erie-Lackawanna serve New Jersey residents and commuters in Rockland and Orange Counties in New York State.

The Long Island Railroad, which transports about 90,000 commuters to work daily, is by far the most important railroad in the region. In fact, it is the largest commuter railroad in the nation. The Hudson and Harlem divisions of the Penn Central carry about 34,000 people per day into Grand Central Station; the New Haven branch brings in 26,000. The other Penn Central lines, which terminate at Pennsylvania Station, carry 48,000 commuters daily. The remaining commuters carried by other New Jersey lines must transfer at either Newark or Hoboken to complete their journeys to Manhattan.

Suburban railroad operations are geared to peak-hour traffic, with most equipment utilized to capacity for only 20 hours a week. Crews, on the other hand, must be paid for a full week's work. On the whole, approximately 70 percent of all commuter railroad patronage constitutes peak-hour loading.

Federal and state regulation has kept passenger fares on regional suburban railroads from rising to a level necessary to cover all applicable operating costs or to provide adequately for maintenance expenditures, to say nothing of replacement of obsolete equipment. The railroads have had no motivation either to deploy top-flight management or to invest in modernization as long as they have been confronted with a losing venture for which there were no apparent offsetting advantages.

The inability or unwillingness of commuter railroads to replace obsolete and worn-out equipment with modern rolling stock was apparent on all the commuter lines serving New York City. A Tri-State Transportation Commission study in 1963 revealed, for example, that of the 3,079 cars operated by the major carriers of the metropolitan region, 64 percent of the 2,016 on New York–Connecticut lines and practically all of the 1,063 cars on the New Jersey railroads were over thirty years old.[1] At that time, it was estimated that replacement of all overage suburban railroad equipment would have cost about $260 million.

By 1969, the equipment situation had become more acute. When the Penn Central took over the New Haven system, it inherited more than 100 cars that were more than forty years old. Twenty had to be scrapped immediately. The New Haven locomotives were not in much better shape. Their unreliability was illustrated by the need for Penn Central to circumvent a New York State law barring diesel locomotives in New York City terminals and tunnels because of recurrent breakdowns in the electrical propulsion systems of the worn-out engines.

The results of trying to run a commuter railroad with old equipment show up particularly in very cold weather, when worn-out rolling stock and other equipment break down more frequently.

During the month of January 1970, less than two-thirds of all trains on the Hudson, Harlem, and New Haven divisions of the Penn Central arrived at their destinations on time, that is, within five minutes of scheduled arrival. For the year as a whole, only 79 percent of all such trains arrived on time.

Similar conditions prevailed on the Long Island Railroad. In 1968, after three years of Metropolitan Transportation Authority operation, the Long Island Railroad showed the poorest on-time record since 1947. This condition worsened during the first half of 1969. Sanguine expectations that capital "infusions" and new equipment would bring about dramatically improved conditions were not realized. These disappointments can be attributed primarily to a labor slowdown, which aggravated an equipment shortage. Because of the sorry condition of the old rolling stock, management had to gamble that new equipment would perform according to the manufacturer's claim. Unfortunately, cars were late in delivery and defective upon arrival.

Simultaneously, shop union personnel, resistant to maintenance

---

[1] *Railroad Suburban Equipment Status Report,* May 1963.

innovations that would have increased productivity, instituted a slow-down, and repairs dropped to practically zero. Late trains and cancellations soared, and the on-time record during the summer of 1969 fell sharply. Since then, following a Metropolitan Transportation Authority accommodation with the unions, car-shop repair rates have shot up, train cancellations have been virtually eliminated, and service has improved markedly. The on-time performance during the first half of 1971 averaged almost 95 percent. At that time new and improved cars were arriving at a rate of from 6 to 8 per week, and by the summer of 1972 the new car fleet had grown to 770.

The labor and equipment problems illustrated by the experience of the Long Island Railroad have relevance to all the region's suburban lines. Operating costs will continue to rise because personnel will seek greater benefits, such as the pension provisions won by members of the Transport Workers Union in 1968. Resistance to labor-saving innovations will probably remain adamant. The strategic role of mass-transit personnel makes it extremely difficult to resist their demands. In the interest of keeping operating costs from becoming open-ended, this problem is one which demands judicious and persistent attention.

BUSES   Metropolitan area bus service provides direct links to Manhattan's central business district, and about 227,000 commuters ride the buses directly into the city each morning. Another 300,000 people use the buses to get to mass-transit systems to complete their journey to work.

Three major bus systems operate in the metropolitan area. The New Jersey buses bring about 71,000 commuters into Port Authority terminals between 7 and 10 A.M. each weekday morning. The New York City Transit Authority operates virtually all the local bus lines in Brooklyn and Staten Island, about half of the service in Queens, and a few lines in Manhattan. The Manhattan and Bronx Surface Transit Operating Authority (MaBSTOA), a subsidiary of the Transit Authority, operates most of the local lines in the Bronx and Manhattan. Transit Authority buses carry 1.4 million fares each day, while the daily load on MaBSTOA lines is about 1.0 million.

Private companies carry 10 percent of the city's riders. Recently, some private lines, running express buses between central Manhattan and the city's outskirts, have provided a new quality service, which has drawn increasing patronage. The Transit Authority also has instituted express bus service running from Staten Island into both

Manhattan and Brooklyn as well as express service from Queens to Manhattan. Express routes from the Bronx are currently under study.

In New York City, the fares set by the Transit Authority are uniform for publicly owned buses. Buses have been more heavily affected by fare changes than have subways, showing a greater decline in patronage when the fare goes up. For example, when a 10-cent fare increase was put into effect in 1970 on both subways and buses, subway patronage declined by 4.7 percent, but, bus patronage fell by 7.8 percent.

As in the case of subways, the bus system depends primarily on passenger fares for revenue, and labor costs account for most of the total operating expenses.

The problem of deficit operations plagues the various bus systems, as well as other mass-transit modes. In New Jersey, where intrastate route losses have persisted during a period of increased interstate patronage, the Department of Transportation is investigating the possibility of a public takeover of lines and the provision of operating subsidies. In New York, most of the Transit Authority and MaBSTOA buses in Manhattan and the Bronx operate at a small profit, while lines in the other boroughs incur deficits. The private lines have been operating in the black.

PATH The Port of New York Authority owns and operates the Port Authority Trans-Hudson Corporation (PATH), formerly the Hudson and Manhattan Railroad. This rapid-transit facility provides the major rail access to the Manhattan central business district from Newark, Jersey City, and Hoboken, as well as a link between Manhattan and the New Jersey suburban railroads. PATH carried 39 million passengers in 1970.

In 1962, following passage of legislation by the states of New Jersey and New York, PATH was created to acquire, operate, and modernize the bankrupt H&M Railroad. Since then, PATH has spent about $130 million for property acquisitions and capital improvements. The entire PATH program, eventually totaling $200 million, embraces the design and purchase of a new fleet of about 300 air-conditioned cars, construction of a new terminal at the site of the World Trade Center in lower Manhattan, construction of a Transportation Center at Journal Square in Jersey City, and thorough rehabilitation and renovation of other equipment and facilities.

The PATH system demonstrates how the problem of peaking contributes to deficit operations. The reason lies in the living patterns of the suburban rail commuters and in the fewer passengers carried in nonrush-hour service provided by the suburban railroads of New Jersey. As a consequence, about 70 percent of all PATH traffic occurs during the peak rush hours. Moreover, peaking within the peak occurs. Almost half of all passengers who travel between 4:36 and 5:36 P.M. board the trains during the 18 minutes beginning at 4:45 P.M. In an effort to ameliorate this situation the Port Authority has helped to sponsor a promising staggered work-hours experiment in the financial district. In 1970, PATH incurred a deficit of $13.2 million.

STATEN ISLAND RAPID TRANSIT

The Staten Island Rapid Transit system operates from Tottenville to St. George along the eastern edge of the island. It carries approximately 17,000 people a day. The city purchased the line at a cost of $3.5 million from the Baltimore & Ohio/Chesapeake & Ohio Railway, and effective July 1, 1971, the Staten Island Rapid Transit Operating Authority, a wholly owned subsidary of the Metropolitan Transportation Authority, assumed operational control of the line.

New York State, through the Metropolitan Transportation Authority, and New York City are planning to rehabilitate the line and have made a commitment to purchase 52 new air-conditioned cars during 1973. The state has committed $18.75 million for modernization, and the city will pick up the rest of the cost which will total about $25 million.

AIR TRAVEL AND ACCESS TO KENNEDY INTERNATIONAL AIRPORT

In addition to its role as the hub of the nation's major metropolitan region, New York City also serves as one of the great transportation centers of the world. The front office of corporate America must be in constant contact with the rest of the nation and the rest of the world. Thus, the trip between Manhattan and the airports serving it assumes great significance and must be considered as part of the "market" for transportation services.

At present, the bulk of this demand is met by private or quasi-private vehicles such as buses, taxis, and limousines. However, congestion in Manhattan, at the airports, and in between has increased. This situation undoubtedly will worsen in the coming years. Some 20 million passengers used Kennedy in 1967; 40 million are expected to do so in 1975. Furthermore, the airport continues to grow in importance as an employment center. Jobs at Kennedy are expected to double in the next fifteen years from their present level.

Early in 1968, the Metropolitan Transportation Authority, the Port of New York Authority, and the airline industry began cooperative efforts toward developing direct rail service to Kennedy. The objective was to permit high-speed transportation between the airport terminal and Manhattan with connections at Jamaica for Brooklyn, Queens, and Long Island points. In 1971, the New York State Legislature passed a bill directing the Port Authority to finance a Kennedy Airport rail connection in New York and a Newark Airport link in New Jersey. An identical measure was approved by the New Jersey Legislature. Engineering designs for a 17.4-mile high-speed rail line from Penn Station to JFK Airport are expected to be completed by the end of 1972. The access route of the new facility, which will provide nonstop service between mid-Manhattan and JFK, will include a currently unused portion of the Long Island Railroad.

TRANSPORTATION CENTERS An important part of the Metropolitan Transportation Authority's regional plan involves the creation of transportation centers. Combining auto-parking facilities with accessibility to rail or bus commuter lines, as well as local taxi service, the transportation centers also have the potential for development as commercial-activity clusters. Current plans envision the creation of such centers in Rockland, Westchester, Putnam, and Dutchess Counties on the northern tier, as well as on Long Island in the vicinities of Great Neck and Hicksville. In addition, a major transportation complex is planned for the midtown area, probably centering around 48th Street.

THE DECLINE AND RISE OF MASS TRANSIT

ECONOMICS OF MASS TRANSIT The economics of mass transit embraces two major elements: the large amount of capital required for modernization and expansion of facilities, and the demonstrated inability to meet constantly rising operating costs through the fare box. With very high fixed costs, relatively rigid fares, and restricted ability to trim variable costs in accordance with fluctuations in passenger volume, mass transit as a business presents an inescapable "loss" situation.

The principal reason for the financial difficulties of mass transit is the drastic decline in the total number of riders, accompanied by a sustained concentration of travel during the four or so hours associated with the journey to work. Peak-hour loading, which determines the extent of capital and labor inputs in mass-transit rail facilities, constitutes 55 percent of the traffic on subways and 70 percent on the suburban railroads. After the 5-cent subway fare increase of July 1966, a 2 percent drop in passengers during the regular weekdays was accompanied by a 4 percent decrease in Saturday traffic. By time of day, a drop of 2.4 percent took place in the hours from 7 to 10 A.M., but it was 8 percent from 10 to 12 A.M.

The pattern of traffic loss on suburban railroads is evidence of the predominance of the automobile for all local transportation except for the core-oriented journey to work. No real competition exists between the private passenger car and the trains or buses for off-peak-hour transportation. In such a situation, judging by the transportation patterns that have developed, increased satisfaction and convenience outweigh any traffic congestion that might dissuade drivers from using their vehicles.

The dispersion of population to outlying areas of the city and the metropolitan region, poorly served by mass-transit rail facilities, has further increased the disadvantages of mass transit vis-à-vis the automobile. To a great extent these demographic trends have been reinforced by the large amounts of federal funds available for highway expenditures in urban areas. The federal government provided $2.2 billion for highway aid in fiscal 1970, most of it requiring only 10 percent in matching funds from the local governments. On the other hand, only $175 million was provided for public transportation, and this required a one-third matching by local governments. This disproportion has led planners, local governments, and voters in the direction of highway rather than public-transit solutions to urban transportation problems. Thus, the body politic, which has fostered the growth of road traffic over the years, will have to shift emphasis if the region is to achieve a modern transportation system that depends more on the potential efficiency of mass transit.

On the revenue side, regulatory and political pressures have kept fares too low to meet operating costs, let alone replace obsolete equipment (to say nothing of providing an adequate return on investment in the case of private carriers). The historic judgments of regulatory agencies continue to impose severe burdens on today's mass transit. Long after it had become patently invalid, railroad regulatory commissioners apparently acted on the assumption that suburban rail carriers exercised a monopoly and that it was a privilege to transport passengers. Accordingly, private railroads have been forced to sustain loss operations. Unrealistic regulation has had its inevitable result in declining quality of service and equipment, as well as bankruptcy in some cases. Within both the public and private sectors of mass transit, the strenuous efforts to hold fares down by curtailing the growth of operating expenses have imposed inordinate restrictions on management flexibility and have led to short-range "savings" incurred at

long-run costs to riders of poorer service and enhanced personal danger, as recent mass-transit accidents and fires have shown. By the early winter of 1970, the long-range disinvestment process and consequent equipment deterioration had contributed to some of the most serious service breakdowns ever suffered by the city and the region.

Despite the political and regulatory resistance, transit operators have been permitted to raise fares from time to time. Although rate increases thus far have generated additional revenues, they have diverted traffic to automobiles and have reduced mass-transit patronage without generating a significant reduction in operating expenses and still have failed to cover ever-soaring operating costs. Fare increases within the subway system have exerted a particularly regressive impact on the central city's low-income population. In addition, they have caused the greatest relative erosion in short-haul, off-peak traffic. They have, therefore, impeded the efficient utilization of capital equipment.

PUBLIC PRICING   One goal envisioned in the improvement of mass transit involves the diversion of automobile drivers and passengers to public carriers. The provision of free highways and streets, combined with selected river crossings that either are free (such as several over the East River) or have tolls that have been stable for thirty years, not only diverts a limited amount of patronage and revenue away from mass transit but also contributes to the city's automobile saturation. Port Authority Hudson River crossing tolls, for example, were 50 cents at a time when subway fares were only a nickel. Now subway rides cost seven times as much, while the Hudson bridges and tunnels still charge the same half dollar. Peak-hour traffic, moreover, is encouraged by a 50 percent reduction in price on commutation tickets.[1]

The need for enhanced support of balanced regional transportation facilities suggests the appropriateness of imposing higher and economically more reasonable charges for the use of highways and river crossings.[2] It may be expected that some diversion to mass transit will occur as a result of such action; its major impact most probably would be the transfer of badly needed added revenues to mass-transit use.[3] For example, only about 10 percent of work trips to Manhattan

[1] Early in 1970, traffic flow across the Hudson was expedited by a new "one-way toll" system which doubled the toll eastbound and eliminated it completely westbound.

[2] With respect to the Port of New York Authority, statutory and contractual restrictions limit its support of rail mass transit effectively to PATH.

[3] The doubling of tolls on the Ben Franklin Bridge across the Delaware River at Philadelphia brought about an estimated auto-traffic reduction of about 5 percent, while the subsequent introduction of the Lindenwold-to-Philadelphia suburban rail service added another 3 percent to the auto-traffic diminution.

are made by automobile, and it is generally conceded that this demand would not be very sensitive to any driving-cost increases resulting from additional tolls. In addition, much of the vehicular traffic traversing bridges and tunnels is destined for places other than Manhattan. That ratio is about 50 percent for Hudson River crossings. Auto traffic makes up less than one-fourth of vehicular trips on Manhattan streets, trucks and buses another fourth, while taxis account for the remainder. Moreover, about 27 percent of all private auto commuters to the Manhattan central business district come from Manhattan itself, only 11 percent from west of the Hudson. The remaining 62 percent come from the other boroughs of New York City, Westchester, and Long Island.

New York City had investigated the feasibility of adding to the mass-transit revenue base by charging tolls on those East River bridges which are now free. Failure to secure the required state approval has killed the idea, for the time being. Although politically difficult, adoption of this procedure would be consistent with the recent increase in the tolls on the Triborough Bridge and other facilities of the Triborough Bridge and Tunnel Authority.

Mass-transit revenue can be supplemented from such sources as increased bridge and tunnel charges or a gasoline tax. Nevertheless, these funds would still fall short of making up the full deficit on all the mass-transit lines. It is difficult to envision any adequate additional source of subsidies other than direct support from all levels of government.

CAPITAL INPUTS AND OPERATING SUPPORT
A major requirement for overcoming years of neglect and achieving a high-quality network is a "massive infusion of new capital." Regional mass transit is receiving a good portion of the needed capital infusions, primarily as a result of planning at the Tri-State Transportation Commission and the $2.5 billion New York State bond issue of 1967, especially designated for use throughout the state. These actions have not only provided substantial state funds for improving mass transit, but, along with the creation of the Metropolitan Transportation Authority, have served as devices for assuring the maximum flow of available federal funds into the region. In addition, New Jersey has passed a transportation bond issue of $600 million, and further sizable sums will continue to be provided out of New York City's capital budget. The federal government, moreover, is to offer limited financial assistance for capital investment in mass transit in a new five-year program which will provide contractual authority for the expenditure of $3.1 billion throughout the nation.

The enormous regional needs, however, estimated on a first priority basis at more than $2 billion for New York City alone, and excluding normal annual subway replacement and modernization costs of about $100 million, dwarf the apparent level of capital availability. The 1971 New York State transportation bond issue would have provided $1.35 billion for mass transportation—approximately $800 million of which would have been used for improvement and expansion of the city's subways, but it was rejected by the voters.

Nevertheless, the region has an advantage over other large metropolitan areas in that it already has mass-transit facilities and rights of way in place. The subway system alone has an estimated value of approximately $8 billion.

Although the capital requirements of mass transit are far from fully met, the problem is closer to solution than that of making up operating deficits. The prospect of supporting mass-transit operations out of the general public treasuries, for example, meets with resistance because there is a perceived distinction between the interests of users and of the general public. Mass transit apparently has not achieved the status of a universally beneficial service automatically meriting public support. That some facilities remain in private hands further complicates the issue. Strong, if waning, feelings persist against further operational support, engendered in part because of the already large contributions, but also because of the fear that new funds will encourage union contract demands and may simply compensate for inefficiencies.

The reluctance, or inability, of public officials to provide adequate operating support has had serious effects on the goal of efficient resource allocation in the region's mass-transit industry. Age has been the Transit Authority's major yardstick for determining the condition of equipment as well as its need for replacement. The important point, however, is not how old a car may be, but how well it has been maintained and whether it costs more or less to maintain available equipment in good condition than to replace it with new stock. Relatively little for upkeep, but millions for new equipment, has become the inadvertent result of restricting major subsidies primarily to capital accounts. Within the city's subway system, for example, preventive maintenance has suffered and equipment has been allowed to break down before being sent to the repair shop.[1] This is a consequence

---

[1] New York City Transportation Administration Report, "Inspection of City Owned and State Operated Mass Transit Facilities," Jan. 5, 1970. The MTA claims, however, that there has been ameliorative action, particularly since the beginning of 1970.

of the arrangement under which maintenance expenses fall within the operating rather than the capital sphere.

A NEW ERA IN MASS TRANSIT Chronic traffic saturation and the accompanying pollution of the atmosphere have tended recently to temper America's love affair with the automobile. While private passenger cars remain the predominant mode of transportation for most uses, their applicability to the journey to work in concentrated central business districts has become less and less feasible. Residents of metropolitan areas throughout the United States have come to the realization that the toll of smog, dirt, delays, accidents, and ugly roadside development has begun to outweigh some of the advantages of personal transportation. Rapid-transit systems are being constructed, planned, or revitalized all over the nation. In truth, there is a growing awareness that if rail mass transit did not exist, it would have to be invented.

Early in the 1960s, the Tri-State Transportation Commission, an interstate planning agency charged with the responsibility for defining and solving transportation and related land-use problems of the New York metropolitan region, conducted a comprehensive planning operation designed to update the aging mass-transit facilities of the entire region. By 1965, their strategy involved improving service on existing suburban lines rather than planning new ones. This meant that modernized equipment, extended electrification, and direct delivery to Manhattan (especially from New Jersey) could yield the greatest improvement in service to an expanding population for the dollars invested. Although recognizing the potential growth of population in the areas outside New York City, the major thrust of Tri-State's plans lay in catching up with the past.

With respect to the city's rapid-transit system, however, improvement of service was to be directed not to an expanding population but to one that was rearranging itself. Therefore, subway improvements required investment in some new lines and extensions to relieve overcrowding.

Two major transportation emergencies in recent years have led to public action of far-reaching consequences. Both involved the public takeover of essential rail lines which, under private ownership, had reached advanced stages of decay and were on the point of complete collapse. The first occurred in 1962 when the Port of New York Authority was persuaded to assume ownership and operation of the Hudson and Manhattan Railroad, now PATH. For the first time, automobile-generated funds were applied to the rehabilitation and operation of a commuter rail facility. A similarly decrepit condition existed with respect to the far larger and more vital Long Island Railroad when New York State purchased it in 1965 and assigned its operating responsibilities to the then Metropolitan Commuter Transportation Authority (subsequently the Metropolitan Transportation Authority).

It is hoped that response to crisis rather than plan will become less frequent in this region. The states of New York, New Jersey, and Connecticut have structured organizations and programs which may involve the eventual outlay of about $1.5 billion over the next decade for modernization of the region's suburban rail network and an additional $2.3 billion (with New York City participation) for improvement and expansion of the city subway system.

The largest of these programs by far is currently being pursued by the Metropolitan Transportation Authority. Presented in 1968 after the voters of New York State had approved the state transportation bond issue, the master plan for mass-transportation improvements in the New York portion of the metropolitan area is one of the largest and most comprehensive urban transportation programs ever devised. It involves among other things the construction of a dual-purpose tunnel under the East River at 63rd Street; extensive expansion and modernization of the subway system; a half-billion-dollar renewal program for the Long Island Railroad (including the purchase of 770 new cars) and the New Haven (in cooperation with the Connecticut Department of Transportation), Hudson, and Harlem divisions of the Penn Central; refurbishing of the Rockland County and Orange County portions of the Erie-Lackawanna Railroad; creation of a Metropolitan Transportation Center in east midtown Manhattan, as well as transportation centers elsewhere in the region; rehabilitation of the Staten Island Rapid Transit Railway; construction of a spur of the Long Island Railroad to Kennedy International Airport; and the development of crosstown "people movers" at 48th Street and in the financial area of downtown Manhattan.

In New Jersey, the state Department of Transportation, which anticipates sharply increased patronage on its suburban rail lines, plans to allocate over $200 million of bond subscription funds to modernize the Penn Central, Erie-Lackawanna, and Jersey Central Railroads, in addition to an expected $125 million in federal funds. New Jersey provides not only capital but also operating subsidies to the commuter railroads, which will remain in private hands. In New York, on the other hand, the Metropolitan Transportation Authority was created as a device whereby the public could assume complete ownership and operation of transportation facilities such as the Long Island Railroad or enter long-term lease arrangements with the Penn Central for operation of its Hudson and Harlem divisions.[1]

FEDERAL ASSISTANCE TO URBAN MASS TRANSIT

Federal aid for urban mass transit was initiated in 1961. The Housing Act of that year included provisions for demonstration grants as aspects of integrated plans for community services. The Urban Mass Transportation Act of 1964 authorized a three-year program of loans and grants for capital improvements and a program of research, development, and demonstration grants. The program limited any state to 12.5 percent of the national appropriation, with the federal share set at 66.6 percent, assuming the preparation of comprehensive urban transportation studies.

As the 1964 program developed, the inadequacy of both the amount and the extent of federal support for urban mass transportation became increasingly apparent. Transit interests began to lobby for a trust-fund arrangement, similar to that established for the federal highway program. Instead, the Nixon Administration proposed in August 1969 "contractual authority"[2] as a means to provide the kind of long-term assurance of federal support required before local governments could commit themselves to the large-scale investments needed in mass transit.

The legislation signed by President Nixon on October 15, 1970, provides for a federal commitment to mass-transit aid programs of $10 billion over a twelve-year period. The bill will furnish graduated contractual authority during the first five years up to $3.1 billion to finance new and improved mass-transit systems in urban areas in addition to loans to states and to local public bodies for the acquisition of real property required for urban mass transportation. The bill sets limitations of 12.5 percent for any state, although densely urban states like New York can compete for up to 15 percent of the total federal allocation in any given year. The federal share of capital investments is limited to 66.6 percent. Applications have already been submitted by New York for 750 air-conditioned subway cars.

---

[1] Two forms of state-mandated taxation help support the Metropolitan Transportation Authority's mass-transit operations. These include station-maintenance costs for surburban railroads imposed on the respective municipalities and a portion of the mortgage recording tax.

[2] Contractual authority confers upon an agency legal authority to obligate the sums which become available each year. The authority is not technically dependent on prior congressional approval, although Congress can cut back the amounts that can be obligated regardless of the rhetoric in the act itself. Appropriations are still required each year to provide the cash necessary for liquidation of obligations.

Although the annual appropriations contemplated in the act are small relative to the total authorized, the law's backers assert that they are consistent with the lag between the obligations and disbursements experienced under any major construction project. The effect of the new program of contractual authority would be to make possible the start of essential projects requiring several years for completion, with the assurance that federal financial assistance would be available to complete the project in accordance with the terms of the contractual obligation. With contractual authority set at $3.1 billion, the total accruable to New York State will range between $390 million and $465 million. This region may well receive the lion's share of that amount. The inadequacy of this aid, which must be spread throughout the state, is revealed by the fact that even the larger amount is less than what is required to rehabilitate the Long Island Railroad alone.

In addition to the innovation of applying contractual authority security for long-term transportation planning and investment decisions, the Urban Mass Transportation Assistance Act of 1970 embraces one provision of far-reaching consequences. One section declares that:

> *The Secretary of Transportation shall conduct a study of the feasibility of providing federal assistance to help defray the operating costs of mass-transportation companies in urban areas. . . .*

Federal participation in operating subsidies would constitute a significant departure from established policy and promises potentially important help in offsetting some of the fiscal difficulties in mass-transit operations, particularly in the New York metropolitan region.

REGIONAL MASS-TRANSIT OPERATING AGENCIES

Any review of the mass-transit facilities in the New York metropolitan region reveals considerable variations in operations and management. To some extent, these reflect diversities in transit needs. For example, the operation of suburban facilities poses a different set of problems from those involved in running the New York City subway-elevated system. Even within the suburbs conditions vary.

Achieving the desirable cooperation among regional transportation operating agencies faces formidable obstacles. Regional transit systems operate in three states, under several forms of ownership, and benefit from a variety of subsidy arrangements. These differences make it extremely difficult to conduct operations so that they contribute as much as possible to the ideal of a unified system. Although it has been suggested that a single "super" regional authority might best achieve coordination among modes, it is doubtful that any one organization could satisfy the diversity of transportation needs which regional differences in political jurisdictions and traditions impose. Political realities, moreover, indicate that during the foreseeable future the current alignment of the region's transportation authorities will prevail.

To a large extent, the objective of a consistent long-range course of action has been promoted in the New York area by the creation of the Metropolitan Transportation Authority, which now has responsibility for policy direction and control of the most important of the mass carriers—the city subway and bus system and the Long Island Railroad. In cooperation with the Connecticut Transportation Authority, arrangements have been made for a Metropolitan Transportation Authority takeover of the New Haven and, in principle, also the Hudson and Harlem divisions of the Penn Central. When these plans are consummated, substantially all regional passenger rail service east of the Hudson will fall within the planning and policy aegis of the Metropolitan Transportation Authority. That agency, together with the Port of New York Authority, which owns and operates PATH, and the New Jersey Department of Transportation, which has working subsidy arrangements with commuter railroads on the west shore of the Hudson, will constitute the institutional structure for a regionally oriented mass-transit network.

The necessary policy cooperation among New York, New Jersey, and Connecticut occurs through frequent contacts among the respective agency heads as well as through more formal negotiations. In addition, the Tri-State Transportation Commission provides a forum for transportation planning and is the central regional agency for review of federal-aid allocations. Once the operating-agency administrators reach a policy decision, they appoint interagency task forces to work out details of the agreements. Exemplifying this is the cooperation of the Tri-State Transportation Commission, the Port Authority, the New Jersey Turnpike Authority, and the New Jersey Department of Transportation on the Urban Corridor Demonstration Program project to experiment with exclusive bus lanes on the Route 3 approaches to the Lincoln Tunnel. Another task force may try to determine the allocation of Pennsylvania Station facilities between the competing commuter needs of traffic from New Jersey and Long Island. The Metropolitan Transportation Authority has been awarded $14.8 million for a development project to build eight prototype self-propelled, gas-turbine, electric-rail commuter cars.

One of the most perplexing difficulties confronting regional and state political administrators is the creation of transportation authorities whose structure embraces the proper balance between the degree of independence necessary for operating efficiency and an adequate responsiveness to changing public needs. An independent agency, for example, may elect to undertake only those projects which promise a profitable return, or at least are self-supporting.

On the other hand, to the extent that an operating authority remains overly dependent on public fiscal support, it is subject to excessive political pressures. This not only results in capital misallocations, but also leads to political interference with management prerogatives on issues such as fare structure and labor relations. The Port of New York Authority, much admired for the smoothness of its operations, can function efficiently largely because it is self-supporting. By contrast, the facilities currently within the Metropolitan Transportation Authority domain are unlikely to furnish any net surplus, even with the Triborough Bridge and Tunnel Authority's automobile-generated revenues. The Metropolitan Transportation Authority cannot, therefore, expect to enjoy any measure of freedom of action that is generated by prosperity.

If local and state governments were dedicated to the creation of an independent transportation operating agency of maximum effectiveness, they would create a structure as financially independent as feasible. This could be accomplished partially by including within the agency's domain facilities earning surpluses sufficient to offset some portion of mass-transit operating losses. Provision of capital funds adequate for necessary service expansion and modernization could follow from a trust fund such as exists in the federal government with respect to highways. If this were too much for local governments to accept, they might utilize the method under consideration with respect to federal mass-transit capital assistance by creating a kind of supplemental local contractual authority—leaving to the operating agency (with appropriate responsibility safeguards) the discretionary power of deciding when and how to invest such funds and to set fares.

CONCLUSIONS

MONEY The atmosphere of politics and emotion enveloping mass transit in the New York area emphasizes the need for dispassionate analysis. A lack of consensus on goals, performance standards, criteria for investment, and sources of revenue aggravates the highly charged situation.

An obvious ingredient for an improved system is more money. That will have to come primarily in the form of public subsidies. The beleaguered mass-transit operators have faced understandable difficulties because of limited funds. This problem is compounded, however, by an irrational accounting system which, in effect, provides operating authorities with an incentive to treat capital as a free good. Despite the best intentions, such a system has inevitably fostered under-maintenance and excessive capital consumption. The distinction between sources of capital and operating funds is apparently responsible for the continuation of this faulty budgeting. It should be discarded in favor of a method that takes full costs into account and then allocates the costs between the riding public and the responsible political jurisdictions. Failing that, it should be possible at least to make whatever legal adjustments are required to transfer specified maintenance expenses into the capital account.

Imposing additional demands on capital funds currently or potentially available for the region's mass-transit facilities may, however, endanger a program whose fate is already far from certain. Much will depend upon the extent of federal commitment to mass-transit aid. Certainly the legislation currently under consideration will not provide funds adequate to compensate for the inadequacy of local fiscal resources. The state and the city, moreover, may reduce their contributions by the amount of capital subsidies received from the federal government, or use the funds for other purposes.

The apparent inability or reluctance on the part of the public to pay the costs of sustaining mass-transit services in prime condition affects all management decisions, exerting a special impact on maintenance. Recent subway and commuter railroad accidents and fires illustrate one unfortunate ramification, however tenuous the association may be in specific cases. Responsibility for subway safety falls clearly on the Transit Authority. This does not, however, mean that it alone should bear the blame. Much of the fault rests on public indifference and the failure of political leaders to stress the need for providing adequate revenues to the transit operators.

The newly aroused public interest in quality of mass transit should stimulate a strong and successful effort on the part of the Metropolitan Transportation Authority and the Transit Authority to obtain more substantial support. If unable to provide adequate maintenance within the constraints of their income, these agencies should sound a loud and clear warning concerning the consequences of inadequate maintenance and should convey the message that the public can get only what it pays for.

LABOR   The problem of dealing with organized labor in the transit industry has assumed enormous importance. Labor costs, which constitute over 90 percent of operating expenses, will continue to rise inexorably because of union contract demands and organized labor's resistance to productivity-enhancing innovations. This takes on added impact with public assumption of responsibility for the formerly privately operated commuter railroads. This action, in effect, induces railroad-union members to seek the same package of benefits now enjoyed by members of the Transport Workers Union, whose contract provisions are by far the most important ingredient in the constantly rising operating costs of the subway system. One cannot expect, moreover, that there will be any slackening in the pace of demands for pay increases, particularly while inflation remains a problem. Management will have to exert every effort to develop a wide variety of sophisticated techniques to make collective bargaining work, to sustain labor's good will, and thus to assure stability in mass transit. One important route to achievement of these objectives would be to run a customer-satisfying operation, which would promote employees' *esprit de corps*. The "service-breakdown/passenger-hostility/employee-resentment" syndrome must be reversed. Establishment of appropriate incentives for quality performance would also help to promote stability. Unions, for their part, will have to exercise a greater degree of responsibility to compensate for the great power they can wield. Without resolution of the problem of mounting labor costs the burden of supporting transit services threatens to become an open-ended cost situation. Obviously, this will be one of the thorniest problems for any transportation system of the future.

FARE STRUCTURE   The role of good management is not only to attain harmonious labor relations, but also to achieve maximum efficiency in all phases of operations. For example, all suburban railroads (and to a lesser extent the subways) face the same difficult problem of utilizing resources economically as a result of peak-hour loads and the absence of an appreciable volume of traffic at other times of the day and on weekends. Attempts thus far to attract additional commuter patronage during off-peak hours have not met with any great success. What seems to be required is the ability to support more frequent service and exploit more fully a flexible rate structure that would recognize the low extra cost involved in hauling such additional traffic. Special incentives and rewards to management for successful resolution of this problem would seem appropriate. With respect to the subways

and PATH, the current staggering of work hours in the financial district of Manhattan is a significant step in the right direction. Incentives in the form of fare reductions for off-peak hours conceivably could promote this idea.

There are other flexible fare innovations which merit close examination. The subway system must bear a heavy cost burden because long-haul passengers are transported at the same charges as those applicable to short distances. Apparently, this state of affairs has not resulted in any experiment designed to develop ways by which an equitable zonal fare arrangement might be worked out. A Transit Fare Committee was created recently by New York City, ostensibly to study the problem, but there seems to be no sense of urgency to remedy the inequities.

TECHNOLOGICAL INNOVATIONS

The region has a large investment in mass-transit facilities, and it is important that the system be modernized thoroughly. A major impediment to significant technological or systemic changes in the subways seems to rest on the interrelations of each segment with other parts of the system. For example, the concept of using three of the four available tracks for traffic in the prevailing rush-hour direction could not be instituted, according to the Transit Authority, because there is no way of avoiding a pile-up of trains in Manhattan where storage space is inadequate.

Certainly the subway system should be automated wherever possible in order to exploit the capabilities of modern computer technology. For example, a computer system could promote the automation of nonpassenger operations where economies are possible, without objection from the public because of the danger of malfunction. But perhaps, in view of the unlikelihood of revolutionary changes in a large fixed plant with extensive and complex interconnections, the major thrust of innovational efforts should be in developing and introducing equipment with greater comfort, reliability, and ease of maintenance and operation.

ACCOUNTABILITY AND EFFICIENCY OF TRANSPORTATION AUTHORITIES

It is vital that managements of public transportation be held strictly accountable for proper and efficient operation of facilities under their control. This is especially important because of the lack of any corrective market influence on the public transportation monopoly.

Probably the most effective method for ensuring accountability of transportation authorities would be through periodic reviews in depth by ad hoc commissions of experts appointed by the Legislature and empowered to probe into all phases of the agencies' operations. The commissions' reports could be used by the Legislature or the Governor to institute any necessary remedial action. It is hoped that these reviews would be conducted in the spirit of common goals of the reviewing commissions and the authorities with respect to safety, proper maintenance, good labor relations, overall management efficiency, and receptivity to innovation.

BUSINESS INVOLVEMENT   In the early and supposedly unsophisticated days of American economic development, entrepreneurs recognized the relationship between the transportation facilities such as turnpikes, canals, and railroads and the subsequent promise of profit, based not so much on the operation of the facility as on the expected appreciation of land values and the heightened level of economic activity in the area served. Accordingly, there was not as much pressure for immediate returns on the transportation investment. Public subscriptions frequently helped pay for the creation of the transportation mode, and public-private cooperation was recognized as a legitimate means for creating the transportation necessary to make possible the economic development of an area.

The need for society as a whole to take such a broad view of public transportation is even more acute today than it was in the past. The business community, working with government, should cease to view public transit as a thorn in its side, or even as merely a job of moving masses of people between home and job. Certainly it is in the interests of good business to improve the public receptivity to the need for more adequate support of mass transit. With respect to investment opportunities, new transportation centers should offer substantial retail facilities as well as transportation. Other opportunities for business lie in the development of air rights over rail yards such as those in Sunnyside, Queens.[1]

New transportation and business complexes could not only benefit the community, but also generate revenue for the transportation operator. These complexes could be established either in the suburbs, or at Manhattan locations such as along the Second Avenue subway line, on the proposed 48th Street transit route, or in the financial district. The latter could give rise to modern above- and below-ground shopping plazas attractive enough to substantially improve the quality of the affected neighborhoods. These developments will require consid-

---

[1] In this connection, it should be noted that New York City has established a Transit/Land Use Committee to evaluate development opportunities along the new transit rights-of-way and to produce land-use, zoning, and urban design proposals.

erable resources and management skills and they merit thorough study.

In sum, mass transportation should not be considered in isolation, but as a vital link connecting people and jobs. Businessmen are concerned with the well-being of business and residential areas. They must become more concerned with the transportation systems that enable these areas to flourish. As a corollary, coordinated planning and cooperation between government authorities and the private sector will enhance not only the transportation system but also the prosperity of the region the system is intended to serve.

Environmental Quality and New York City

So far discussions have focused upon problems that directly affect the individual. We have seen how public policy can help establish livable income levels and attempt to provide relevant education, adequate housing, or reliable transportation. Public policy as expressed through the bureaucracy shapes and molds, but the role of government in social issues has been traditionally that of provider rather than stern enforcer. Citizens still choose their own life style, even if in so doing they deny themselves vital services.

But environmental issues may change this. Environment by definition is a collective noun, and measures protecting it could imply withdrawal of individual rights and sacrifice of personal wants. The apparatus for controlling the environment could prescribe new criteria for pollutants or mandate limits on services to citizens. Conceivably, that apparatus could project governmental authority to new levels.

The improvement of the quality of the environment is an enormous and complex task. The solution to one pollution problem sometimes creates another. And since much of what is now considered threatening to physical and economic health is not new but only newly recognized, the prospect that still other threats will appear is not

unlikely. Then too, there are questions of relative costs. As the work goes forward, it becomes increasingly apparent that, while everybody must pay something, there are choices that must be made among conflicting political, social, and economic factors.

WASTE DISPOSAL AND POLLUTION

Pollution is nothing new. Nearly every human activity produces residue of some sort. Cutting a piece of wood leaves sawdust, washing one's hands creates dirty water, and simply breathing produces carbon dioxide. Nature has an enormous capacity to assimilate and neutralize waste material. But in recent decades, as cities and their surrounding areas have become more densely populated, as industrial processes have grown increasingly complex, and as the nation's living standards have reached ever higher levels, disposing of the inevitable residue has become a major problem.

In Western countries, the discharge of untreated human and industrial sewage into the waterways and the discharge of gaseous waste into the air now seriously disturb the public, whose mood has changed drastically in just a few years. Only a short time ago, from Pennsylvania to Northern Italy, people in mining towns and factory cities accepted dirt and stench without question or complaint. Today, even the Japanese seem to have reached their limit, though they still often live amid conditions of pollution that most Americans would not tolerate.

The problem has become acute because the normal economic forces that actively help determine social behavior have not been brought to bear on waste-disposal decisions. The rivers, seas, and air have been readily available free of charge for use as public dumping grounds. Since the producer of waste tries to rid himself of it as cheaply as possible, these seemingly costless facilities have been employed as a matter of course. The best way to correct the consequent abuses, as will be seen, is to harness the powerful forces of the marketplace, which until now have been absent.

THE ECONOMICS OF POLLUTION

Pollution is an injustice because, while people have no direct vote in the waste-disposal decision, they may be directly affected by the result. Whenever an individual imposes an undesired burden upon others, the total, or social, costs of his actions exceed the costs he must bear privately. Ending this divergence between social and private costs is the key to pollution control.

A familiar example of cost divergence is the factory that dumps its wastes into a river at no cost to itself and contaminates the drinking water of communities downstream. There are many other, more ordinary examples of individual actions that produce detrimental side effects: the person who smokes a cigar in a crowded room; the suburbanite who, to the dismay of his neighbors, raises chickens on his front yard. Costs such as these are common to our everyday world; the point at which they become a problem depends upon the amount of harm caused to others and the number of persons affected.

Pollution is a major problem today, not because of some moral failure of our society, but because our economy does not compel polluters to assume the costs they inflict upon others. In our economic system, market prices play a crucial role in directing the exchange of scarce goods and services. But since the rights to air and water are usually either vaguely defined or held in common, no one need pay for them. Thus, since the effective price of air and water is zero, there are no market constraints on their use. The result is unchecked waste disposal and unacceptable pollution levels.

In most instances, the marketplace is quite capable of bringing producers and consumers face-to-face with the full social costs of their behavior. For this to happen, however, present laws and customs which perpetuate the freedom to dump waste into the environment would have to be revised. At present, polluters are generally free to pollute without having to compensate society for injury. When legal recourse is available at all, the harmed party is burdened with bringing suit and proving damages, and even when class-action suits are possible, the cost of organizing a community may be prohibitive.

Moreover, some kinds of damage are difficult or impossible to prove or even to measure. The expense is easily recognizable when air pollution causes respiratory ailments or more frequent repainting of houses, or when pollution forces communities to spend more on water purification. Recognition is more difficult when the leaching of landfill, for instance, damages the ecological system of a marshland. Some costs are intangible, such as the loss occasioned by the destruction of natural beauty. Other costs, more concrete, are simply the aggravation of naturally occurring ailments such as asthma, or of naturally occurring processes such as metal corrosion. In addition, when several sources emit pollutants simultaneously, attribution to a single source is often difficult.

If those wishing to dispose of waste into the environment had to bear
the entire social cost, things would be different. Polluters would have
strong incentives to cut their emissions, thus closing the gap between
private and social costs. This would require limitations on common-
use rights to environmental resources such as water and air—either
by setting a price on such use or by limiting the use by decree.[1]
Ideally, environmental property rights could be restructured to make
market pricing practical. It is clear, however, that at this time government administrators prefer direct regulatory involvement to reliance
upon indirect pricing measures.

Pollution standards or bans on certain emissions or practices will
no doubt reduce damage to air and water every bit as effectively as
would a system of user fees. But since these regulatory practices
depend ultimately upon the political process, they have a major weak-
ness. As a general rule, air and water resources will be used more
efficiently and society will be better off when polluters reduce their
emissions to the point where the cost of further abatement equals
the cost of pollution to others. Under a one-man, one-vote system,
however, people are unable to state the intensity of their prefer-
ences—that is, the magnitude of their costs—as they can when voting
with dollars. Government regulators thus lack the cost-benefit information that is provided automatically and continually in an efficient
marketplace. In consequence, regulators cannot allow for differences
in control costs among sources of pollution.

The importance of this distinction is illustrated by the results of
a study undertaken by the U.S. Public Health Service in Kansas City
several years ago. Under uniform abatement standards, the study
calculated that particulate matter in the air would drop by more than
one-half to 85 micrograms per cubic meter of air at a cost of $26.4
million. Under an alternative abatement scheme that accounted for
differences in the costs of pollution control as well as differences in
plant locations in relation to wind patterns, particulate levels would
have dropped to 86 micrograms per cubic meter—just 1 microgram
more—at a cost of only $7.5 million. In other words, a 1-microgram
increase in air quality would cost nearly $19 million!

Direct regulation might be an efficient alternative if society wanted

---

[1]Placing limits upon the use of common property resources is not an unusual
function of government. In some cases, rights have been reduced by direct edict—
Federal Communications Commission allocation of radio frequencies is an illustration.
In other cases, government has simply set prices—parking-meter fees help allocate
scarce parking space, for example.

to reduce pollutant emissions to zero, but only rarely will that be the case. Overuse of air and water for waste disposal has produced the present levels of pollution. But a regulatory scheme that caused underuse could be equally damaging to the overall well-being of society. The fairest, most efficient way to determine the best level of use is to attach prices to environmental resources.

One way to do this is through "effluent charges," or taxes on waste. In the past, many environmentalists have objected to such taxes as "licenses to pollute," but they are beginning to realize that such controls can be adjusted to cut pollution while preserving the benefits of an efficient economy. Another persuasive consideration is that with pollution charges the incentive to reduce pollution remains even after regulatory standards are met. Taxes ensure that efforts to develop less-expensive control devices will not cease.

Although environmental regulation by fiat appears to be here to stay, this should by no means preclude schemes that will bring market forces to bear upon appropriate environmental problems. Indeed, an eclectic approach to environmental management will undoubtedly prove more fruitful than one narrowly conceived. In those instances where a market solution is not practical, regulation should aim to guide decisions along the same lines as would the market, by carefully considering costs as well as benefits.

In the following sections, current efforts to upgrade the environment of New York City are assessed in terms of the foregoing economic principles. These principles not only apply to pollution abatement, but are generally applicable in all cases—such as the provision of mass transportation, education, and parklands—where markets function poorly or not at all.

WATER POLLUTION AND SEWAGE DISPOSAL

WHERE WE ARE

The waters around New York City are polluted mainly by human waste. Industrial-waste disposal is no small problem, but it is much smaller than in many other waterways across the nation. The sewage burden imposed on the city's waterways is enormous. The principal rivers of the New York region serve a population of roughly 15 million and all converge within a 20-mile radius of the Battery. This is the largest "population shed" of comparable geographic area served by a convergent drainage system anywhere in the United States and one of the largest anywhere in the world.

Human waste is organic in nature and decomposes readily in water

through bacterial action, but in doing so, it consumes the oxygen dissolved in the water. If sewage decomposition consumes enough oxygen, fish and other aquatic life cannot survive, and further waste decomposition produces foul gases such as hydrogen sulfide and methane instead of innocuous carbon dioxide.

Compared with other cities across the nation, New York City does a respectable job of treating its sewage. Thirteen treatment plants process more than 75 percent of the total flow before dispersing it into the waterways. The rest drains untreated from Manhattan into the Hudson and from Brooklyn into the East River. After treatment, New York's sewage uses up only 25 to 30 percent of the oxygen it would have otherwise. Even so, the total amount of treated and untreated sewage discharged by the city consumes as much oxygen as would the total untreated sewage generated by a city the size of Chicago.

To add to the problem, the New York sewer system combines both sanitary and storm flows within the same pipeline network. This arrangement works well in dry weather, but after heavy rain or snow the treatment plants cannot handle the load. On the forty or so days a year of storm runoff, excess sewage drains directly into the waterways with no treatment whatsoever.

But even if New York City solved all its sewage-handling problems, pollution of the area's waterways would not stop because New Jersey dumps at least as much waste into the water as does New York City. A large portion of northern New Jersey's waste is handled by the Passaic Valley Sewage Commission (PVSC), which collects it from Newark and twenty-eight other communities in four counties, an area of 3 million poeple and 700 industrial plants. A large portion is inorganic industrial waste that does not break down as readily as organic sewage. And the effluent that PVSC discharges into Upper New York Bay off Bayonne is not nearly so thoroughly treated as is that of New York City.

Despite the burden placed upon the waterways of New York Harbor, water pollution has actually declined in the past decade by one significant measure. New York City's Water Resources Administration (and previously the Department of Public Works) has conducted a harbor pollution survey annually since 1909.[1] (See the accompanying

[1]Harbor water is sampled at a number of locations (only the East River and Hudson River points are shown here) and analyzed to determine the volume of oxygen dissolved in the water in comparison to the amount that would be present under unpolluted conditions. Decomposition of organic material uses large volumes of oxygen: the more oxygen, the less pollution.

DISSOLVED OXYGEN SATURATION

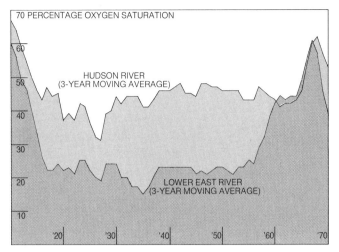

SOURCE: New York City Department of Water Resources.

chart.) The survey shows that oxygen levels decreased rapidly from 1909 until around 1920 and then held fairly constant until the early 1950s in the case of the lower East River and until the early 1960s in the case of the Hudson. The subsequent improvement has been dramatic. There are, in fact, reports that certain species of fish are returning to the East River after decades of absence. Little direct, short-run correlation seems to exist between the installation of new sewage plants and the upward movement in levels of oxygen. Still, there is not much doubt that the improvement of the past dozen years is due to a general upgrading of water-treatment facilities throughout the area.

WHERE WE ARE HEADED Beginning with the Federal Water Pollution Control Act of 1956, the nation has aimed at explicit water-quality targets. In fifteen years little has been achieved, but now the barriers to improvement are rapidly giving way and forward momentum is in danger of carrying water purity to extremes. The Federal Water Pollution Control Act Amendments of 1972 sets as national goals the total elimination of pollutant discharges into navigable waters by 1985 as well as interim targets—the "protection and propagation of fish, shellfish and wild-life" and "recreation in and on the water"—by 1981.

If this language is to be taken literally and all waterways are indeed to be swimmable by 1981, the implications for New York are considerable. New York City presently plans thirteen major pollution control projects, including two entirely new sewage-treatment plants. If the city holds to its plan, all dry-weather sewage will receive treatment at a higher level than is presently attained and the waste load imposed on the surrounding waters will be halved by the late 1970s. While the problem of storm-sewer runoff has not yet been fully solved, a prototype treatment plant is planned for Jamaica Bay in anticipation of a program of citywide construction. But even if these extensive plans are successfully carried out and the storm-runoff program is greatly accelerated, multipurpose waterways such as the East and Hudson Rivers are still unlikely to be suitable for swimming.

But more importantly: *Should* they be made suitable for swimming? Investment in water quality is subject to diminishing returns. That is, each succeeding improvement in the quality of water benefits society less than the previous one. Thus, at some point, higher quality water becomes a poor investment. For New York, that point seems likely to be reached while water quality is still somewhat lower than the goal set by federal law.

As dirty as the surrounding waters are, they are not a major health hazard. Since New York City's drinking water is drawn from reservoirs, some of which are more than 100 miles north, there is no chance of contamination from the waterways around the city. Although infected shellfish have caused outbreaks of hepatitis, more stringent shellfishing regulation has greatly reduced chances of recurrences. Even though a sharp reduction in water pollution would allow local shellfishing to resume, this scarcely appears worth the expense.

The most important benefits that would arise from an improvement in New York's water quality are associated with better recreational opportunities such as those proposed for the Gateway National Recreation Area. What is it worth to prepare New York's waters for swimming, boating, and sport fishing?

While such a question is not easily answered, there are some indications. The greatest factor in favor of such an effort is the enormous number of people concentrated within reach of the shore. But this tends to be offset by other considerations.

Any proposed new recreational investment must be considered as part of the total array of recreation opportunities offered to New Yorkers. They have many facilities to choose from, such as Jones Beach, the Jersey shore, and the Catskill Mountains. Many who now prefer these spots would not benefit significantly from the recreational development of the New York waterfront. Furthermore, heavy use of a water-oriented project in the New York area is limited by the climate to three or four months a year.

In addition, the cost of developing a full-scale recreational area would be extremely high. The official capital-cost estimate for New York City's pollution-control projects alone is just over $1 billion, and this may be far too low because of soaring construction costs and unforeseen complications. For example, the estimate for the proposed North River sewage-treatment plant more than doubled recently, from $350 million to $750 million, and this revision alone brings the total city expenditure necessary to $1.5 billion. The New Jersey contribution has also been estimated at around $1.5 billion, and this figure likewise is probably understated.

Even if $3 billion would buy water of the quality demanded by federal law, clean water is of little use unless people can get to it. The government would have to acquire and develop large areas of shore property, often at the sacrifice of other productive uses for it. Adequate access routes would have to be built from population centers too, including mass-transportation facilities. Then, to make New York Harbor suitable for large-scale pleasure boating, the 300 abandoned piers and 2,000 sunken wrecks that litter the harbor would have to be cleared away. The waterfront wreckage is a navigational hazard as well as an eyesore.

It would also be necessary to curtail dumping waste materials into the outer reaches of New York Harbor. At present almost 8 million tons of assorted wastes are dumped there each year. These include construction and demolition debris, coal ash from steam-generating plants, contaminated dredge spoils, and sewage sludge. The disposal area is already termed a "dead sea," and signs are increasing that damage is spreading to beaches nearby. Little is known of the effects of an increasing volume of such debris, but the Council on Environmental Quality has strongly recommended an early stop to the ocean dumping of sewage sludge and polluted dredgings. If this happens, New York City will have to bear the added expense of disposing of these materials in other, more costly ways.

All in all, it would cost many billions of dollars to develop a full-scale recreational facility around New York's waters. The benefits from it have to be balanced against this tremendous cost, and when this is done, the weight of evidence does not seem to support proposals that would require an overall pristine purity. A moderate increase in water quality would be in the public interest, but the desire for cleanliness should not seriously impede the multipurpose use of New York Harbor. New York's well-being may depend critically on its success in remaining a seaport, with its waters acting as a conduit for waterborne traffic as well as a dumping place and a recreation site.

In the face of all these powerful, conflicting demands, the way to determine the optimal use of New York's waters is through a new reliance on the interplay of market forces.

The easiest market scheme to implement might be a system of "environmental usage certificates" for ocean dumping in the area, as suggested in the 1971 Economic Report of the President. This system would limit the amount of dumping directly, but allow the price for dumping to be set indirectly.

Under this plan, the federal government (probably represented by the Corps of Engineers) would determine the capacity of the ocean off the Lower Bay to assimilate different wastes. It would then issue usage certificates, or dumping permits, specifying the type and amount of waste, with the total amount licensed not to exceed the natural limit of the waters. If the government auctioned off these certificates to the highest bidders and allowed private resale, a price would be established for this use of the waters.

Since the prices that bidders are willing to pay measure the costs of alternative waste-disposal methods, this method would ensure that the scarce waste-disposal resources in that area of the ocean were being put to their most productive use. The beauty of this system lies in its simplicity and flexibility. There would be no room for haggling over water-quality standards or their measurement. Administrative overhead could be kept to a minimum, and the revenue derived from the sale of certificates could be applied to other environmental needs.

More importantly, the certificate procedure would in no way conflict with the dynamics of the economy. In a healthy economy, costs and prices are constantly adjusting to fluctuations in underlying supply and demand. Over time, the preference of waste producers for ocean dumping privileges will undoubtedly change. As this occurs, the market for dumping rights will allow certificates to be bought and sold at mutually agreeable prices that will continue to reflect the value of this use of New York's waters.

An intriguing aspect of this arrangement is that persons or organizations who desire minimal or no ocean dumping would have the opportunity to achieve this end. They could buy up usage certificates and simply withhold them from the market. This would not only reduce the total amount dumped but would also raise the price of all remaining certificates and thus make ocean dumping even more expensive.

Since the federal government has clear authority over offshore waters, there are no real legal obstacles to applying this scheme to ocean dumping. But legality becomes a serious (though not insurmountable) obstacle in the case of inland waterways, especially those bordered by more than one state, as is the Hudson. In such cases, a system of effluent charges might be more practical, with fees based on the social cost per weight or volume of pollutant. Costs would go down as less waste was discharged, giving polluters an incentive to reduce their pollution.

Effluent charges have the same advantages as do environmental usage certificates. They automatically adjust for differences in pollution-control costs among pollution sources, and they do not interfere with the vital and continuous shifting of resources throughout the economy. In addition, such charges provide a strong abatement incentive for most polluters and thus would act quickly to curb waste discharges. With charges properly set, they achieve the elusive goal of saddling polluters with the full social costs of their actions.

CHOOSING A STRATEGY

Total reliance on the marketplace, however, cannot solve all water-pollution problems. In general, if the damage caused by a pollutant cannot be measured easily, or if the amount of damage rises sharply as the discharge increases, then direct regulation may be more attractive. Since market-oriented solutions tolerate deviations in the quantity of pollutants emitted, such schemes become less workable as the cost of deviation increases. If even a small increase in quantity is dangerous to life, specific limits or flat bans are probably the most appropriate methods of control. For example, the toxic metals mercury and cadmium would not be satisfactorily controlled by a system of market forces. In New York's waterways as elsewhere, regulation of pollution should not be wedded to any one procedure.

CONSERVING AIR RESOURCES

THE SCOPE OF
THE PROBLEM

Pollutants in the air may be dispersed either horizontally by wind or vertically by rising air currents. The New York region benefits from generally strong winds. The 13-mph average windspeed at LaGuardia Airport is stronger than that reported by 90 percent of the nation's Weather Bureau stations. The winds are often accused of foisting New Jersey's pollution upon the residents of New York City, but the problem has been much exaggerated. By far the largest portion of the pollution that plagues New York originates within the city limits, and the wind on the whole is a disperser rather than a bearer of outside pollutants.

New York also generally enjoys favorable conditions of vertical

mixing. Occasionally a layer of air at an upper level will be warmer than that below it and will act as a "lid," preventing vertical air movements. This is known as a temperature inversion condition. In general, the lower the inversion layer, the worse the pollution. Fortunately inversions under 500 feet in altitude are less frequent in New York than anywhere else in the country except the New England coast and southern Florida. New York averages only two major periods of stagnation a year, while Atlanta, for instance, averages ten.

Despite mostly favorable weather conditions, New York City experiences continual and often severe air pollution. The large number of sources and contaminants alone greatly complicates any attempt to reduce atmospheric pollution. Incinerators, generating stations, heating plants, automobiles, and airplanes all contribute to the problem.

The best available evidence suggests that common pollutants aggravate preexisting diseases of the lungs and heart as well as minor but annoying respiratory ailments, and, in addition, may be associated with certain types of cancer. Several studies have claimed to discover statistically significant relationships between air-pollution levels and "excess" deaths during New York City pollution episodes. Another recent study estimates the national annual cost of health damage due to air pollution to be $35 billion, or about $175 per capita.

In addition, pollutants cause substantial property damage. In 1968, the U.S. Public Health Service estimated property-damage expenses due to air pollution in New York City at $195 per resident. This figure included damage to clothing, homes, and vehicles, but did not consider harm to vegetation, the costs of incomplete fuel combustion, or the deterioration of works of art. These combined figures indicate that the annual air-pollution burden on New York City could be as much as $3 billion—or more than 5 percent of the annual income of city residents![1]

Motor vehicles produce more than 75 percent of the city's gross tonnage of air pollution. But this figure is misleading. The differences among the physical effects of various pollutants make it necessary to weight them according to the damage they are presumed to cause to health and property. For instance, carbon monoxide must be present in a concentration many times that of sulfur dioxide before posing a comparable health problem. Because carbon monoxide accounts for 80 percent of motor-vehicle emissions by weight and sulfur dioxide

---

[1] While other estimates generally range downward from this figure, few authorities could deny that air pollution is an extremely expensive phenomenon.

less than 1 percent, it is unlikely that the automobile is responsible for any more than half of New York's air-pollution damage.

Many people wrongly believe that air pollution from motor vehicles is increasing rapidly in New York City. In fact, it is rising as a percentage of all air pollution, but only because total levels are declining while it holds steady. Because traffic has reached a near-saturation level in the city, there are only limited increases in vehicle-miles driven and, therefore, in exhaust emissions. But vehicular emissions are still a serious problem, especially since they contribute indirectly to irritating photochemical smog.

EMISSION CONTROL Because motor vehicles are not tied to a permanent location and because they are regulated mainly by state governments, it is hard to limit their discharge of waste into the atmosphere—particularly in New York City, where many out-of-state cars enter and leave daily. Consequently, it would be hard to administer a system designed to make a car owner pay a fee based on the actual amount of pollution emitted. But emission standards, such as those set by the federal government, will work much the same as the fee system because they will force the car owner to pay for pollution-control devices.

With auto use in New York City relatively stable, pollution-control devices required to satisfy federal standards should gradually reduce the level of exhaust pollutants in the city's atmosphere. But while Congress has ordered auto makers to reduce exhaust emissions by 90 percent in 1975 and 1976 models, no plan exists for upgrading the exhaust systems of older autos. At present attrition rates, unequipped models will not be replaced on the road to a significant extent for at least ten years. Without strong legislation there is little reason to expect auto owners to install antipollution equipment voluntarily. General Motors test-marketed an antipollution kit in Arizona during 1970. Despite intensive promotion and a cost of only $20 including installation, only 528 kits were purchased, although 334,000 vehicles were estimated to be eligible. General Motors reluctantly canceled the program.

With or without controls, the pollution generated by a car depends critically on the operating condition of its engine. Even with the proper hardware, effective reduction of pollution requires frequent, intensive inspection to promote better engine maintenance. Recognizing this, New Jersey plans to put teeth into its emission standards by setting up a comprehensive system of exhaust inspection. A 30-second test designed to weed out gross offenders is scheduled for each

of the 3.3 million registered motor vehicles in 1972. Vehicles failing to have major defects corrected within two weeks may be banished from the road. In the first two years of inspection, repairs may cost New Jersey motorists $55 million.

Such an inspection system would be difficult to transfer to New York State. New Jersey conducts its regular car-safety inspections at thirty-three special facilities, while in New York such inspections are conducted at 10,800 privately owned, state-licensed service stations. New York would either have to install expensive inspection equipment at these stations or introduce a system of special pollution-inspection centers. It might be more practical to use the California system of roadside spotchecks, administered by either New York City or the state.

TRANSPORTATION PRICING The output of car exhaust can be cut in another way—by limiting the number of vehicle-miles driven. This may be accomplished directly by bans and restrictions, or indirectly by increasing the cost of owning and operating a motor vehicle. But such ideas will not be acceptable politically or economically if the total price the public pays for transportation rises significantly. Improvement and extension of the mass-transit system must be a major element in any long-range plan to curtail the use of autos in New York City. In fact, the twin goals in the city's fight against air pollution must be to develop a modern system of mass transit[1] and to launch a set of measures discouraging the use of cars.

One such deterrent measure (which would also raise funds for mass transit) would be to boost tolls on bridges and tunnels into and out of Manhattan and to collect tolls on those that charge none. Another deterrent would be to increase the cost of parking in Manhattan through extended parking bans, higher garage taxes, and strictly enforced parking regulations. Emission charges could be approximated by collecting registration fees calculated on the basis of horsepower. An additional indirect tax on emissions could be levied by putting an extra tax on gasoline.

These deterrents, however, are not wholly satisfactory. For instance, the extra gas tax—which is one of the market-oriented suggestions most frequently heard—could be evaded unless out-of-city areas applied the same tax. Nor would this tax differentiate very well between the car with a well-tuned, "clean" engine and the car that spews out

[1]For a more complete discussion of mass transport versus highways, see section on transportation.

a noxious exhaust cloud. Higher tolls on bridges and tunnels could be "evaded" by those who drive only in Manhattan. And the extra auto registration fee would not directly tax the user for miles driven or pollutants emitted.

Full or partial bans on motor traffic in Manhattan have often been advocated. But one strong objection to such bans is that no one really knows how much of the air-pollution burden would simply be shifted to other areas nearby. Likewise, a selective closing of streets could shift more pollution and congestion into parallel routes in Manhattan.

One of the most effective methods to cut down auto pollution quickly would be to clamp controls on taxicab and truck emissions. The city's 14,000 licensed taxis account for half the miles driven in the heavily polluted areas of Manhattan and for about 35 percent of the pollution originating from motor vehicles. Trucks account for an even larger share, about 50 percent, of this pollution. And the greatest portion of this share comes from short-haul vehicles powered by conventional gasoline engines. Long-haul diesel-powered trucks are much less of a problem.

The New York State plan for compliance with federal air-quality standards for the New York metropolitan region proposes conversion of all gasoline-powered taxis and fleet vehicles operating in the central business districts to liquefied petroleum gas (LPG). The installation of an LPG system is fast and cheap, its operating costs are comparable to those of a conventional engine, and, best of all, overall pollution is cut by as much as 90 percent. Unfortunately the city's Fire Code forbids the transportation or storage of LPG within the densely populated areas of New York, even though it is allowed in other cities. If the state's plan is approved, this disagreement is likely to be settled in court. But the idea is sound, based upon proven technology and workable economics.

The ultimate solution to pollution by motor vehicles may yet be the development of an economical, all-purpose alternative to the internal combustion engine. But even in terms of current technology, pollution from autos can be brought to an acceptable level. Like every other type of pollution, this type is due to society's failure to set an appropriate price on the use of natural elements for waste disposal. Every automobile operator has access to the atmosphere which, free of charge, absorbs gaseous waste from his car—while the opportunity to breathe uncontaminated air has become an expensive privilege for the man on the street.

In a number of ways, the social costs of motor-vehicle operation are being shifted back to the operator. The price of an automobile will rise by at least $300 when the hardware necessary to meet 1976 federal standards is added. Motorists will have to pay to keep their cars in better operating condition, and they will have to pay, directly or through taxes, the cost for inspection equipment and its operation, as well as stiffer tolls on highways and bridges. In addition, they may pay nonmonetary costs in the form of less convenience and longer commuting time. These costs are not negligible. But they do seem to fall within the range of a reasonable settlement for a sizable social debt.

THE ELECTRIC POWER DILEMMA

Throughout the past decade, sulfur dioxide headed the list of major air contaminants in New York City. In 1965, eleven Consolidated Edison generating stations inside the city caused 40 percent of New York's sulfur dioxide emissions, with the rest resulting from the heating of large commercial and apartment buildings. Soon thereafter, the City of New York began campaigning for a limit on the sulfur dioxide content of fuels. By December 1967, nearly four years ahead of the deadline set by the city, Con Edison began burning fuel with a maximum 1 percent sulfur content. Similar progress was made in space heating, and as a result of these efforts, by 1970 the amount of sulfur dioxide vented to the atmosphere had been cut nearly 60 percent. Con Edison has continued to reduce the sulfur content of its boiler fuels since 1970; if shortages of low-sulfur fuels can be avoided in the future (a highly uncertain prospect), conditions should improve still more.

While progress has been rapid, ground-level sulfur dioxide readings remain well above proposed federal standards (see chart), and on a "damage caused" basis, sulfur dioxide still accounts for a substantial portion of the city's air-pollution burden. In 1966, Con Edison and the Office of the Mayor of the City of New York entered into a "Memorandum of Understanding" in which, among other things, Con Edison accepted "the principle that, to the fullest possible extent, power from coal- or oil-fired plants should be generated outside City limits." It was then thought that the construction of a new generating capacity, mainly nuclear, outside New York would allow Con Edison to phase out gradually its older, less efficient operations in the East River area, thus easing air pollution.

No one correctly anticipated the difficulties which have been encountered since then in the creation of a remote generating capacity. The Cornwall Pumped Storage plant has been rescheduled for 1980

ANNUAL AVERAGE SULFUR DIOXIDE CONCENTRATION

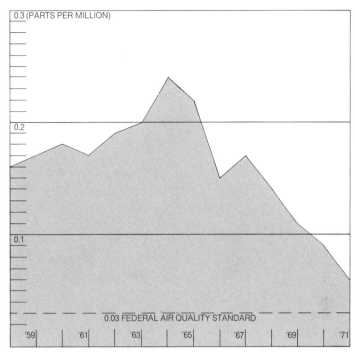

0.3 (PARTS PER MILLION)

0.2

0.1

0.03 FEDERAL AIR QUALITY STANDARD

'59 '61 '63 '65 '67 '69 '71

(121st St. Laboratory, Manhattan)
SOURCE: New York City Department of Air Resources.

in the face of strong conservationist protests. Two new nuclear plants at Indian Point have been delayed, partly in response to environmental objections. With construction schedules slipping and power demands rising rapidly, Con Edison felt that the only way to retire the old plants while retaining a safe reserve margin was to add new base-load capacity to an existing plant. The resulting proposal to expand the Astoria (Queens) plant evoked strong public reaction, both pro and con, during the summer of 1970.

Despite a growing demand for electrical energy, the efforts to reduce pollution have made new generating facilities less and less acceptable in or near the city, while rural communities increasingly resent the cities' attempt to "export pollution" in the form of remote generating plants. To some environmentalists, the only solution to the problems of power generation is to limit arbitrarily the quantity generated. But since activities that even they recognize as beneficial—such as sewage treatment, mass transit, and waste compaction systems—require large quantities of electric power, such a simplistic solution is not satisfactory.

209   Environmental Quality

Even though forbidden by federal policy, the ideal solution to the problem could be the extensive use of nuclear generators within the cities themselves. There is no air-pollution problem with nuclear energy, the cost of transmission is minimized, and surplus heat could be used economically. In the case of New York City, such plants could even be placed underground or underwater. Public distrust of nuclear plants, however, presently appears so strong that no plan of this type could be executed. The Atomic Energy Commission and others have made every effort to document the safety of nuclear plants, but many persons, including a few respected scientists, remain unconvinced.

This leaves open only a few lines of short-term action to help cut down the unfavorable side effects of power generation. Since it is so difficult to build new generating capacity, the utilities are under pressure to make the existing capacity more effective and to lessen its adverse impact on nature. One way to do this is to improve regional and interregional coordination of power supply. Better interconnections among utility systems increase the reliability of electrical supply without the construction of additional reserve capacity. Existing equipment could be made more effective, too, were the time pattern of power demand to be altered. Further attempts could be made to stagger work hours and reduce peak-load demand. Peak loads are particularly troublesome in New York City where workers commute largely by subway and other electrically powered transportation. The extension of daylight saving time through the entire year has been suggested as a way to decrease the load surges that occur in after-dark rush hours.

HOW MUCH SULFUR? Sulfur dioxide emissions might be reduced still more by further lowering the sulfur content of boiler fuel, but such a step poses some complicated problems. The availability of low-sulfur fuel is limited by the scarcity of petroleum naturally low in sulfur and by a current general lack of desulfurization capacity. Though demand for low-sulfur fuel may eventually attract sufficient investment to desulfurization facilities, decreases in sulfur are becoming more and more expensive. Con Edison has stated that the cost of going from 1 percent to 0.3 percent sulfur content fuel might be as much as $130 million in 1972, compared with a cost of $20 million a year for a reduction from 3 percent to 1 percent sulfur. Reducing sulfur beyond 0.3 percent could cost much more than it would be worth in many cases.

This is an instance where market forces could be harnessed to determine the most beneficial reduction in pollution. Fuel-oil users would not be required to burn low-sulfur fuel with a certain prescribed content. Instead, they would be taxed according to the amount of sulfur dioxide actually emitted. Each polluter would decide for himself how much to control his output and by what method. The amount of the tax could be calculated so that current air-quality standards would be achieved. But the overall cost to society would be lower than it would be under a uniform sulfur-content rule because the tax would allow for differences in control costs among polluters. An emissions charge could either complement or replace mandatory standards of air quality.

In one way or another, users of electricity will absorb the full costs associated with cleaner production and distribution, and the increase in user prices will automatically limit growth in demand. Over a period of years, the nation has developed a way of life that depends in many ways on cheap power. Electrical power, especially, has been subsidized by the free use of air and water. When this subsidy is eliminated and the price of electricity reflects full social costs, the rise in energy costs conceivably could cause far-reaching changes in life styles.

INCINERATION The most visible and most annoying of atmospheric pollutants is particulate matter (soot, fly ash, etc.). The incineration of refuse in both private and municipal facilities is New York's largest source of particulate matter. Particulate emissions have been declining since 1966 because coal is being used less for space heating and because open burning has been banned. Controls on incinerators have not been a large factor in this decline.

Incinerator control has been unsuccessful because of a long, involved dispute over the regulation of private incinerators. A 1951 amendment to the building code required all new multiple-occupancy dwellings to install incinerators. The city hoped that private incinerators would eventually replace most municipal incinerators, reducing the expense of municipal refuse collection and disposal. By the early 1960s, however, it became apparent that air pollution resulting from both private and public incineration was becoming intolerable. Local Law 14, compelling incinerator upgrading for most apartment houses, was the consequence. Enforcing this law, however, has proved extremely difficult. Not only is tight enforcement costly to the city, but the constitutionality of the law was in doubt for a number of years. Finally, in 1970, the state's highest court, the Court of Appeals, upheld the constitutionality of Local Law 14, and the Department of Air Resources was able to begin the arduous task of scheduling citywide compliance. About one-third of all private incinerators were reported to be in compliance at the end of 1971, with the remaining two-thirds scheduled for upgrading by 1974.

There are roughly 13,500 apartment house incinerators in New York City, of which 80 percent, or 10,800, were to be upgraded under the terms of Local Law 14. The cost of new equipment for these apartment buildings may total in excess of $80 million. In addition, the New York City Housing Authority maintains some 3,650 incinerators, also subject to Local Law 14, and their upgrading will represent an investment estimated at around $20 million. The city must also bear the cost of upgrading its large central municipal incinerators. Of the original eleven city incinerators, three have been closed as beyond rehabilitation and a fourth is scheduled to be shut down. The remaining seven will be renovated at an estimated cost of $12 million.

Local Law 14 is an indirect method of imposing charges for the use of New York's atmosphere. The price of relative freedom from airborne particulate matter is estimated to be about $112 million. Some of this cost will be paid by general taxation, but the main part of it will be borne by tenants in both public and private housing through rent increases or reductions in other services. Full compliance with Local Law 14 would cut particulate emissions to one-third of their 1966 level. The U.S. Public Health Service has calculated that achievement of this goal would save New Yorkers $800 million in cleaning costs alone each year—an excellent return on a relatively small investment.

However, one more item must be added into the cost calculation. Local Law 14 allows small apartment buildings the option of using municipal refuse-collection services as an alternative to upgrading their incinerator. Also, larger apartment houses may install waste compactors instead of incinerators, and while compaction reduces the volume of waste, the mass is unchanged. And, in order to improve the city's air quality, the municipal incinerating capacity is scheduled to decline.

Thus, the cost of particulate air pollution is, in part, to be replaced by an additional burden on New York's facilities for solid-waste disposal. As noted previously, the concern over water quality will probably mean finding an alternative to the ocean dumping of sewage sludge. This is another instance in which the "solution" of one pollution problem simply aggravates another.

While the disposal of solid waste is not a universally important problem at this time, it is rapidly assuming crisis proportions in many densely populated urban areas. New York City generates nearly 25,000 tons of solid waste daily, a volume that is increasing at an annual rate in excess of 4 percent, while the means of disposal are dwindling at an equally rapid pace.

The creation of new land by filling swamps and shore areas with solid waste has been a traditional method of disposal. In fact, 11 percent of the land area of the city has been created in this way, including much of lower Manhattan and both LaGuardia and Kennedy airports. The city currently operates seven landfill sites, including the nation's largest at Fresh Kills on the western shore of Staten Island. But at the present rate of use, the remaining landfill capacity will be completely exhausted by the mid-1970s. Ecologists, moreover, strongly oppose further filling of wetland areas, particularly the inviting expanse of Jamaica Bay.

With solid-waste volume rising rapidly and landfill capacity diminishing, New York must soon decide on a course of action. Plans have now been abandoned for a series of giant incinerators that, a few years ago, were being hailed as the answer to the city's growing refuse crisis. The plan was scrapped because of heightened concern for air pollution and new, higher cost estimates. As yet, no new plan has been unveiled to replace it.

One solution would be to to "export" the refuse. But attempts to arrange the shipment of solid waste to rural areas have thus far failed, mainly because no community wants to be known as New York City's "garbage dump." Another possibility would be the "mounding" of refuse into plateaus possibly as high as 200 feet. But the mounding process is quite expensive, and few communities seem eager to welcome the presence of ugly, unfinished trash mountains for long periods of time.

Private industry has recognized that the sheer magnitude of the solid-waste problem offers opportunity for profit. A number of innovative disposal systems are presently under development. Such methods as pyrolysis, which heats waste materials in an airless kiln to produce combustible gases, tar, and charcoal, are undergoing exhaustive testing in pilot plants. One compaction system under development will convert everything from garbage to refrigerators into high-density cubes weighing 5,000 pounds each.

It may also pay to reexamine the possibility of deep-water landfill.

Since usable property can be created, extending landfill offshore is especially attractive in the New York region where property values are high. This type of filling has generally been considered too expensive because of the precautions necessary to prevent erosion and the leaching of pollutants. However, new methods of preprocessing refuse and of containing the fill material may change relative costs, especially when inexpensive landfill is no longer possible. The area around Hoffman and Swinburne Islands just south of the Verazzano Narrows would be a promising site to begin offshore disposal operations.

In the face of rapid technological change, municipalities must retain their flexibility and conserve their full array of policy options. One possibility for New York City is to play for time by expanding present landfill operations. Prall's Island, off the shore of western Staten Island in the Arthur Kill, is a good prospect for landfill. When developed, the site would cover 3,100 acres and give New York enough dumping ground for several years while various future courses are evaluated.

RECYCLING: AN IMPOSSIBLE DREAM? One of the most promising methods of solid-waste management, still being developed, does not try to dispose of waste. Instead, it aims to prevent waste, by recycling residue back into the stream of production and consumption before it can become waste.

There is nothing radical about the concept of recycling. Its most obvious allure is that it may be used as an inexpensive alternative to present methods of municipal waste disposal. As the costs of other methods keep rising compared with the cost of recycling, its attraction grows. Projections based on the operation of a recycling pilot plant indicate that, by the late 1970s, a recycling system could have a price advantage of as much as $2.50 a ton over conventional incineration. Thus, large-scale recycling is much more than a figment of the environmentalists' imagination.

A second attractive feature is that reclamation can reduce the demands that economic growth places upon several scarce natural resources. Costless waste-disposal privileges have undoubtedly encouraged the depletion of almost all natural resources at a faster rate than is in the best interests of society. Mineral deposits and other depletable resources have finite limits. Although these limits have often been severely underestimated in the past, some day these deposits will simply be exhausted. The conservation of these scarce materials most logically should involve the recovery of as much waste as is economic.

But probably the greatest appeal is that it seems to represent the missing link in the effort to reconcile economic growth with the struggle against pollution. Recycling closes the economic loop between the production of goods and the production of waste. If waste is reclaimed and reintroduced into the channels of production, the output of goods can grow while, at the same time, the output of pollution is diminished.

Enthusiasm for recycling, however, should not obscure the fact that this proposal, like any other, must be considered in the light of specific costs and benefits. While it appears that the present economic system is biased toward the use of virgin material, the objective should be simply to remove the biases, and not to distort the system in the opposite direction. If the market for waste recovery is allowed to function without major constraints, the proper amount of waste will be recycled and everyone will benefit. It is doubtful that the public good would be furthered by the total recycling of all wastes.

CURRENT RECYCLING   Recycling is hardly a new idea. When a material has a high value compared with the cost of its recovery, it does not stay in the waste stream for long. For example, metal fabrication frequently creates waste that is entirely economical to reuse. Generally, it is homogeneous, identifiable, uncontaminated, and produced in sufficient volume to make recovery worthwhile. But these characteristics, which help make industrial reclamation feasible and inexpensive, are usually missing from municipal waste.

Steel and paper are major components of present-day municipal waste. Paper accounts for about 50 percent of it by weight, and steel for about 10 percent. The demand for scrap paper and steel has declined steadily over the past twenty years.

Iron and steel scrap have lost their importance as basic oxygen furnaces replaced open-hearth operations. From an average price per ton of $53.45 in 1956, steel scrap dropped to $25.94 in 1968. Since then the price has risen moderately, mainly as a result of an increase in foreign demand.

In the case of paper, rising labor and transportation costs as well as improved technology for processing virgin pulp have trimmed the proportion of paper recycled from over 35 percent after World War II to below 20 percent currently. As demand declined, the price of scrap paper fell to $16 a ton, compared with $20 to $24 a ton just a few years ago.

PROMOTING RECYCLING   Efforts to expand recycling thus far have concentrated on improving the archaic technology of the scrap business. The basic technical problem is that of efficiently separating the various types of scrap from one another. Several automated separation systems have been developed, and a few are operating rather successfully in pilot plants.

But even with vastly improved technology, large-scale recycling faces an uphill battle. Existing economic policies encourage the use of virgin rather than recycled materials, and these obstacles must be overcome before recycling can become environmentally and economically significant. Several federal programs, while primarily designed to accomplish legitimate objectives, have undoubtedly lowered virgin-material prices and induced greater consumption of these materials than would have occurred otherwise. Consequently, the reclamation of waste materials has been less profitable.

A number of federal agencies aim at developing new markets and more efficient exploration and extraction of natural resources. In addition, the government aids extractive industries through the tax system. For example, practically every mineral carries with it an arbitrarily determined depletion allowance based upon product sales value, which provides tax deductions often exceeding the initial capital costs of exploration and development. Treasury Department figures indicate that total federal aid to the extractive industries (including forest products) in the form of both direct agency support and foregone tax receipts exceeds $4 billion annually.

Yet taxes can be used as either carrot or stick. Proposals for environmental improvement have generally emphasized the punitive use of taxes, while neglecting the other side of the taxation coin—the tax subsidy. At present, tax subsidies by state and federal governments are largely confined to accelerated depreciation write-offs for new investment in pollution-control hardware. In addition, in New York State, air- and water-purification equipment is exempt from the state sales tax (although not from the New York City sales tax).

In some cases, subsidies are also available through the use of tax-exempt bonds to finance pollution-control facilities. The 1968 Revenue and Expenditure Control Act enables municipalities or other government entities to issue bonds in order to purchase pollution-control equipment and lease it to a private corporation. Based upon historical interest-rate patterns, the company leasing the pollution-control equipment would pay an average of 1.5 percentage points higher if it issued a comparably rated corporate bond. Thus, a tax-exempt financing could result in a saving of $3 million in interest charges over the life of a twenty-year $10 million bond issue. In addition, if the lease is drafted in the form of an installment sale, the company can retain the advantages of accelerated depreciation.

Incentives of these types have several drawbacks. One is that marginally profitable firms are frequently unable to take full advantage of accelerated tax write-offs. Yet these firms are often the companies most in need of improved antipollution technology. A second drawback is that the most efficient pollution-control methods often involve internal adjustments of processes already existing rather than investment in new treatment facilities. Thus, such incentives may actually encourage unnecessary and inefficient investment.

A further difficulty with these subsidies is that they are prohibited when "it appears that by reason of profits derived through recovery of wastes or otherwise in the operation of such property, its costs will be recovered over its actual useful life." Restrictions of this type are based upon fears that businessmen will exploit legislation promoting social goals and thus earn windfall profits. Yet such a provision might discourage useful pollution-control programs which provide reusable materials or marketable byproducts. It might make more sense to err on the side of leniency in subsidizing antipollution investments, and tighten up in future years if experience indicates that competition does not squeeze out windfall profits.

Profit enhancement is especially necessary to spur the expansion of recycling. Accelerated depreciation or tax-exempt financing could prove valuable to an industry that needs desperately to introduce new capital equipment. This type of aid, however, would not be enough to put most secondary materials on a competitive basis with their virgin counterparts. To accomplish this would take more drastic action such as gradual removal of some of the subsidies to the primary extractive industries.

The same effect could be achieved, however, through some more easily implemented system of counterbalancing subsidies. One alternative would allow a percentage of the sales price of reclaimed material to be deducted from current taxes—in effect, a "reclamation allowance" paralleling the depletion allowance. If the percentage allowance were calculated to make the price of reclaimed material competitive with virgin products, resources would be transferred to recycling industries and the quantity of waste might be significantly reduced.

Urban solid-waste disposal would receive the greatest benefit from a recycling incentive program. Not only would the tremendous burden of paper disposal be alleviated, but many of the smaller, but troublesome, components of municipal trash would be favorably affected. For example, organic kitchen waste, commonly referred to as garbage, accounts for about 10 percent by weight of municipal refuse. While this is not a large portion, it is a particularly obnoxious type of waste and one which is difficult to handle. Not only is garbage offensive to the nose, but it attracts vermin and contaminates other types of waste to the point where they cannot be recycled.

One way to dispose of garbage is through composting, a process in which bacterial digestion produces an inoffensive fertilizer. Composted fertilizer, however, has never found a viable market in the United States. Sixteen of the eighteen plants built in this country have been closed because of intense competition from inexpensive (and indirectly subsidized) chemical fertilizers.[1] Tax incentives or other subsidies could make composting into a competitive process that would absorb a significant volume of garbage. Glass and plastics are other examples of wastes that could be recycled under more favorable economic conditions.

Recent studies provide ample evidence that the costs of separating waste materials decline rapidly as the volume of waste increases. This suggests that recycling is inhibited by the local nature of disposal responsibility. The federal and state governments are advocating regional solid-waste disposal units which would greatly increase the volume of refuse processed per disposal site and which could conceivably allow material separation at costs considerably lower than have yet been experienced. Regionalization plus recycling incentives could combine to transform recycling into a major industry, and at the same time improve the quality of the environment. Additionally, the elimination of alleged discriminatory practices in scrap transport pricing, municipal zoning, and product labeling could be a strong boost for recycling.

PERSPECTIVE ON
ENVIRONMENTAL QUALITY

A number of general conclusions emerge from the foregoing discussion. The most basic truth, and one that can stand repeating, is that pollution results when a waste producer is not obliged, in one manner or another, to shoulder the entire cost of waste disposal. The principal task of pollution control is to see to it that disposal costs revert to the polluter, but the methods which can be chosen to achieve this objective are distinctly different, both in terms of their ability to encourage environmental quality and in terms of their economic consequences.

---

[1] Improved technology has caused a new resurgence of interest in composting. A modern composting plant that recently opened in Brooklyn is turning out 150 tons of fertilizer per day, and might eventually produce 1,000 tons daily.

Much care was taken to build a case for the application of market-oriented techniques to the problems of environmental degradation. Schemes which attempt to harness the potent forces of the marketplace and bring them to bear against environmental problems have been shown to be not only theoretically attractive but also thoroughly practical. A pragmatic approach to this issue, however, must concede that market forces are not always appropriate. The would-be regulator of the environment is advised to assemble a number of administrative "tools" to be used singly or in whatever combination permits the greatest advancement of the public interest.

Even before a regulatory strategy can be developed, however, the objectives of a program must be examined carefully in the light of associated costs and benefits. Public discussion on uses of the environment have tended to be characterized by excesses of emotional zeal, but today emotions seem to be yielding to rationality, at least enough to permit reasonably objective evaluation of environmental management proposals.

One point cannot be emphasized too often: environmental quality will be expensive. Contrary to popular opinion, the costs of an environmental cleanup will be borne neither by larger corporations nor by the federal government. Environmental quality will be financed by the ultimate consumer, just as he presently bears the tangible and intangible costs of environmental degradation. The methods chosen to limit pollutant emissions will help determine the total costs, but in any case, the relative costs of producing and consuming various goods will change, and these changes will have the potential for inducing expensive economic dislocations.

Examination within the cost-benefit framework of the specific environmental problems confronting New York City leads to several observations. There is a good chance that the net benefit to society of clean water decreases rather rapidly as water-quality standards become so fastidious as to prevent multipurpose use of the waterways. Recreational use of many of the New York waterways simply appears neither feasible nor desirable. At the same time, further investment in air-pollution control seems to have a potentially high social return. The conversion of taxicabs and other fleet vehicles to low-emission propulsion systems and the effective implementation of incinerator controls are particularly appealing as objectives.

Water- and air-pollution control techniques often simply exchange one undesirable situation for another by accelerating the approach of a solid-waste disposal crisis. New York City can no longer depend upon conventional methods of solid-waste disposal and must experiment with unproven but promising innovations. One of the more promising methods of disposal is to recycle a significantly higher portion of the municipal waste stream back into productive uses. While recycling will probably require some special set of economic incentives in order to be effective, this "closed-loop" concept is the most promising for allowing essential economic growth to harmonize with environmental quality in the long run.

Responsibilities and Resources of the City Government

Recurring throughout these studies is the question of how to finance social programs. This generates endless problems because what is involved in the fiscal management of government is a complex balancing of unequals. Revenues are pitted against community needs; neither are rigid quantities, both are politically rooted. Among the problems encountered are how to spread costs fairly for such services as public transportation, or how to introduce efficiency and trim budgets when patronage and expenditure are in some quarters a measure of success. Good fiscal management buys the tools to cure urban blight, and gives people a sense of direction in finding their way out of their difficulties.

The City of New York spent for current purposes almost $8 billion in fiscal year 1971, over three times the level of ten years earlier. Its budget is the largest for any government entity in the nation except the federal government itself.

Despite the dramatic rise in expenditures of New York City, sources of serious dissatisfaction with public services are easy to find. Too many people remain undereducated; too many people who find it difficult to get jobs—or are unable to find well-paying jobs—are poor; there is too much crime, too much garbage on the sidewalks, and too many potholes in the streets. The air is dirty, the beaches are polluted, and more and more frequently subways stall.

City officials contend that their resources are too limited to improve municipal services sufficiently to meet public needs. Indeed, they sometimes claim that municipal resources are not rising rapidly enough to maintain even the existing level of public services in the face of inflationary cost increases.

RESPONSIBILITIES   The city's Expense Budget of almost $8 billion for the 1971 fiscal year, about 50 percent of which was raised through city taxes, was equivalent to almost one-fifth of the personal income of the residents of the city. But large as it is, this budget by no means includes all the financial activities of the city government. It excludes the borrowing to finance capital expenditures, which is accounted for in a separate Capital Budget; it also excludes the finances of the New York City transportation system, except to the extent that mass transportation is subsidized by the city. Additionally, as the Citizen's Budget Commission has pointed out, a number of items appearing in the Capital Budget are more properly considered as current expenditures.

The major public-service programs covered in the Expense Budget are those in social welfare (mainly income support and health), education, police and fire protection, and environmental protection (mainly sanitation).

Where New York City Spends Its Income (billions of dollars) 1970–71

Social Welfare
38%
($3.0)

Education
24%
($1.8)

Police, Fire, and Environmental Protection
13%
($1.0)

Debt,
10%
($0.8)

Other,
15%
($1.2)

Total = $7.8 billion

Real Estate Taxes

27%

($2.1)

State Aid*

30%

($2.4)

*Other Local
Sources*

26%

($2.0)

Federal Aid

17%

($1.3)

Total = $7.8 billion

*Includes special state taxes

The social-welfare and education programs account for over half
of the total outlays. The major part of social-welfare expenditures
is for welfare payments, but there are also special programs for preschool children, foster care for children, manpower training, and
several additional poverty-related activities. In the field of public
health, the city spends a significant amount on hospitals. Neighborhood health centers concentrated in low-income neighborhoods
dispense health services, and mental health services are also provided.

New York also provides police and fire protection. Under the education category, New York operates the largest city school system
in the world as well as an extensive university system. The Environmental Protection Administration provides sanitation services and is
also concerned with protecting the city's air and water from pollution.

Of importance, but involving substantially smaller dollar amounts,
are parks and other forms of recreational activities, subsidization of
the public transportation system, economic development activities;
and the general governmental responsibilities of running the legislative, judicial, and executive branches.

RESOURCES Of the revenue included in the New York City Expense Budget, over
40 cents of every dollar comes from the state and federal governments.
Receipts from two special taxes (on stock transfers and on mortgages)
imposed by the state are turned over to the city in lieu of local taxes.
Most of the intergovernmental revenue helps to finance specific programs. Federal and state aid for welfare, education, and health pur-

	Per Capita Expenditures (dollars)		
	New York City	38 Metropolitan Areas	All Local Governments
Total†	$773.98	$452.19	$363.92
Local schools	156.62	180.01	165.35
Health and welfare	279.24	75.73	49.07
Police, fire, and sanitation	98.90	57.62	40.01
Other	239.22	138.83	109.49
	Per Capita Revenue		
Total†	$828.84	$448.15	$356.29
Intergovernmental	370.25	154.09	129.17
Taxes	359.24	229.39	172.25
Property	213.12	187.61	147.05
Other	146.12	41.78	25.20
Charges and miscellaneous	99.35	64.68	54.87

*Fiscal year. Because of differences in definition, data may not be strictly comparable in all cases.

† Direct general expenditures and general revenues.

SOURCES: U.S. Bureau of the Census, *Local Government Finances in Selected Metropolitan Areas in 1968-69;* U.S. Bureau of the Census, *Government Finances in 1968-69.*

poses totals about 60 percent of city outlays in these areas, but intergovernmental aid specifically for police, fire, sanitation, and other city activities is minimal. The latter programs are therefore substantially more important in city finances than is implied by the budget data.

Of the revenue raised by the city itself, the major portion is collected in the form of taxes. The tax on real estate is by far the most important single tax, comprising about 60 percent of all city tax receipts. The most important of the other levies are on sales and on business and individual income. A small part of the revenue raised by the city comes from charges such as for water supply and for certain health and higher education services.

COMPARISONS WITH OTHER LOCAL GOVERNMENTS

Budgets of local governments in the major urban centers in the United States have certain characteristics distinguishing them from the budgets of smaller local governments. New York, as the center of the greatest concentration of population in the nation, exhibits an extreme case of the characteristics which exist in most "core" cities.

Local public expenditures per resident in New York City are substantially higher than the average of local governments. This is partly the result of the heavy use of city facilities by nonresidents, who, however, make a large contribution to the city's receipts through taxes and charges. The contribution of nonresidents to the city's tax receipts comes about not only through the city's sales and commuter earnings taxes, but also as a result of the taxation of business property which is in part owned by, staffed by, and provides services to nonresidents.

But of greater importance, the city is a major concentration point for the nation's poor, and both the city and New York State have a traditionally liberal voting population. In part because of state requirements and in part through its own initiative, the city makes very heavy outlays for such income-redistributing activities as welfare and public health services. Other elements also making relatively heavy demands on the city budget are the fire-fighting and police forces and a large roster of municipal employees.

Per capita expenditures for local schools are not high by national standards, and so claim a significantly lower proportion of the city budget than is claimed by education in the average local government budget. However, the moderate proportion of total expenditures allocated for the public schools results from the relatively small proportion of the population which is of school age and attending public schools. Per pupil expenditure in New York is substantially higher than the average for the nation.

New York City taps quite heavily all the major sources of revenue, including grants from the state and federal governments. However, the need for large revenues and the great size and diversity of the city's economy both require and permit the city to spread a broad tax net. Its tax receipts are less heavily concentrated upon property taxes than are the receipts in most local governments, where property-tax collections are the overwhelming tax resource. New York is much more dependent upon sales and income taxes, as well as upon a variety of lesser taxes, than are other local governments.

City collections of charges and miscellaneous revenue are relatively high on a per capita basis, although about as important as such collections elsewhere as a proportion of the total budget. The city provides a greater level of services for which charges can be, and are, made than does the average local government. But the level of charges for many of these services in comparatively low.

RECENT TRENDS

EXPENDITURES

The level of expenditures in the Expense Budget of the City of New York tripled in the sixties. This growth came about because of simultaneous increases in the cost of providing services, in the proportion

	Expenditures (millions of dollars)		
	1960*	1970*	Percent Change
Social services (welfare)	$ 254	$1,519	+498
Education (including higher education)	437	1,421	+225
Health services	183	570	+211
Miscellaneous†	382	1,063	+178
Police, fire, and sanitation	338	864	+156
Pensions	204	466	+128
Debt service	377	676	+ 79
Total	$2,175	$6,579	+202

*Fiscal year. Figures for 1970 based on the mayor's budget proposal. Final 1970 expenditures were somewhat higher.

†Mainly general government, transportation, and recreation.

SOURCE: *Pocket Summary of New York City Finances,* Citizens Budget Commission, and unpublished data.

of the population making use of city programs, and in attempts to improve the scope and quality of services.

The most rapidly expanding major programs were those undertaken in the Social Services Department (a part of the Human Resources Administration). The department's outlays for income-support (welfare) and welfare-related activities were budgeted in fiscal 1970 at six times the level of fiscal 1960. The increase in outlays for education and public health services more than tripled.

Expenditures on police, fire, and sanitation programs, which may be labeled as "housekeeping," rose more slowly, with the 1970 figure 2½ times that of 1960. Similarly, debt service and pensions grew at low rates in comparison with the overall budget. The relatively slow rise in debt service reflects the relatively slow rise in capital expenditures made by the city.[1]

Because of the continuing increase in the cost of goods and services, higher public outlays will be required in the future merely to provide a fixed level of public services. Furthermore, a change in the size or composition of the population may require a change in the total of public services just to maintain the existing level of services per eligible recipient. Only after making adjustments for changes in prices

[1]Capital expenditures are made through the Capital Budget, but amortization payments are drawn from the Expense Budget. Under the state constitution, city bonds are payable from first revenues received.

and for what might be termed "population-workload" can it be determined whether funds have been, or will be, available to increase the level of public services per recipient or to improve the quality of such services. The availability of such funds does not guarantee that services will actually be improved, but only suggests that lack of funds is not the major cause of service problems. And since municipal activities are only one part of the total level of activity being undertaken in the city at any one time, availability of such money does not guarantee an improvement in the quality of life within the city. But it is important to know whether funds have been, and will be, available to increase the scope of municipal services, and to determine what fiscal measures may be required to obtain the funds.

THE PRICE FOR CITY SERVICES A rapid increase in costs played a significant role in the overall increase in New York City outlays during the sixties. These costs were driven upward by sharp increases in the compensation levels of municipal employees, which account for about half of Expense Budget outlays. During the decade, changes in the maximum and minimum salaries for the major categories of municipal personnel ranged from 74 to 112 percent. Taking account of the numbers of employees in the several categories, the changes in such salaries averaged about 85 percent. The costs of fringe benefits also rose rapidly. City payments into the pension funds alone increased by over 125 percent during the period.

In addition to salaries and fringe benefits, there are major city expenditures for transfer payments to welfare recipients and for goods. Rising costs affected these areas also. The consumer price index in the New York region rose by 32 percent during the decade, and the price level of goods in the national economy rose by 18 percent. It may be estimated that the costs associated with transfer payments and the purchase of goods by the city increased by almost 30 percent during the period.

Considering the relative importance of the categories of salaries, transfer payments, and the purchase of goods in the city budget, it is estimated that unit costs associated with the goods and services purchased and price-adjusted transfer payments made by the city took an average jump of about 75 percent during the sixties.

Is the sharp increase in municipal costs unique to New York City? In part, the increase in unit costs for city services is attributable to the general increase in prices throughout the country. The relatively great proportion of municipal activity involving the provision of

	Annual Salaries (dollars)		Percent Change	
			Minimum Salary	Maximum Salary
	1959	1969		
Instructional staff				
Public schools	4,500–8,700	7,950–15,150	+77	+74
Higher education	5,600–16,000	11,005–27,900	+97	+74
Patrolmen and firemen	4,475–5,790	9,499–10,950	+112	+89
Sanitationmen	4,050–5,350	8,339–9,871	+106	+85

SOURCE: New York City Office of Labor Relations.

services rather than the production of goods also tends to make its unit costs rise more rapidly than the average. Improvements in productivity are believed to occur more slowly in service fields than in the production of goods.

Moreover, wages in the public sector of the national economy have been rising more rapidly than in the private sector. During the sixties, the average weekly earnings for nonsupervisory workers on private nonagricultural payrolls increased by somewhat over 45 percent. Meanwhile, the average salary of classroom teachers throughout the United States is estimated by the National Education Association to have increased by 71 percent.[1] Available data indicate that between 1959 and 1969 the median entrance salary of policemen and firemen throughout the country increased by over 40 percent and nearly 60 percent, respectively, while the level of maximum salaries in these employment categories is estimated to have increased even more rapidly.[2]

The faster growth in salaries in the public sector may have been necessary in part in order to attract personnel to the expanding public payroll. But even compared with such increases, the rate of increase in the salaries of New York City employees has been rapid.

POPULATION WORKLOAD Municipal expenditures have risen not only because of higher unit costs but also because of increases in the population workload—a factor that describes the change in public-service requirements resulting from changes in the size and structure of the population. Census data show an increase of 1 percent in the size of New York's popula-

[1] *Estimates of School Statistics, 1969-70,* National Education Association, Research Report 1969-R15.
[2] *Municipal Yearbook,* International City Management Association.

tion in the 1960s, to a total of 7.9 million. The total level of employment in the city is estimated by the New York State Department of Labor to have increased by about 5 percent from somewhat under 4.0 million in 1960 to over 4.1 million by 1970. These estimates suggest that there was a small rise in the total number of persons that must be served by the city during the decade.

The age structure of the population has changed in a manner which would tend to increase public needs in the city. The population under age 20 increased from about 30 percent of the total population in 1960 to over 31 percent of the population in 1970. The costs for all the dependent children under the most costly welfare program— Aid to Families With Dependent Children (AFDC)—and almost all education costs are attributable to this group. The proportionate number of aged persons 65 years and over also grew somewhat more rapidly than the population as a whole, increasing from about $10\frac{1}{2}$ percent of the population to 12 percent. This age group, together with young persons, accounts for a major part of the city's health costs and also contributes substantially to the welfare workload. In contrast, the proportion of persons in the broad age group which is the most productive and least costly in terms of public services, i.e., ages 20 to 64, fell from about 59 to 57 percent.

A substantial number of the city's poor persons may almost be considered as being chronically welfare-prone, in that they are in families headed by females. While data are not available for New York City alone, the U.S. Census Bureau estimates a growth of 43 percent in female-headed families with children in all central cities between 1960 and 1970.[1] It is probable that the percentage increase was substantially larger in New York. The greatest increase in numbers of persons on the welfare rolls between 1961 and 1968 in the city was due to the addition of deserted wives. Although solid evidence is lacking, it may be that some of the overall increase in the welfare rolls, particularly Aid to Families with Dependent Children, resulted from an increase in the proportion of persons eligible for assistance who actually have applied for and received such assistance.

In estimating the overall change in the population workload for city services over the decade, it was assumed that the number of persons in homes headed by women and requiring AFDC assistance in New York City grew by 75 percent. It was assumed that the

[1]U.S. Bureau of the Census, *Social and Economic Characteristics of the Population in Metropolitan and Non-Metropolitan Areas: 1970 and 1960,* Current Population Reports, Special Studies, ser. P-23, no. 37, 1971.

proportion of "poor" persons in the rest of the major population age groups did not change, but that the size of the poverty group was affected by the total growth of the population and by a growing aged population. On this basis, the city needed a rise of about 45 percent in social welfare funds merely to account for the increase in its poverty population.

Expenditures for "social welfare" in 1960 accounted for about 20 percent of the total city Expense Budget. However, for estimating purposes, some expenditures for other purposes, such as for education, were taken as being poverty-connected. The public-school-age population, the resident population, and the total working population grew by about 11, 1, and 5 percent, respectively. Taking account of the budgetary costs related to each of these groups—as well as the poverty group—the total of city expenditure needs due to population-workload changes is estimated to have increased by 10 to 15 percent.

New York City Population Characteristics

	1960	1970	1960–70 Percent Change
Total population	7,781,984	7,867,760	1.0
Population age group*			
0–19	30.1	31.4	+1.3
20–64	59.4	56.6	−2.8
65 and over	10.5	12.0	+1.5
Employment†	3,953,600	4,112,300	4.8
	1959	1969	1959–1967 Percent Change
Poverty population:			
Number of families in N.Y.C.	266,000	189,000	−28.9
Number of families in U.S.	8,281,000	4,948,000	−40.2
Percent N.Y.C. of U.S.	3.2	3.8	+18.9

*Percent of total
†Monthly average in fiscal year
SOURCES: U.S. Bureau of the Census, *Trends in Social and Economic Conditions in Metropolitan Areas,* Current Population Reports, Special Studies, ser. P-23, no. 27, 1969; U.S. Bureau of the Census, Current Population Survey; *Employment Review,* State of New York, Department of Labor.

SCOPE AND QUALITY OF PUBLIC SERVICES

On the basis of the data in the preceding sections, it appears that the average increase in the cost per unit of public service provided by New York City in the sixties was about 75 percent and that the population service workload increased by about 10 to 15 percent. Thus, in the sixties, a 100 percent increase in city expenditures for public services from the Expense Budget would have been required just to maintain the level of real services per eligible service recipient.

Placed in relation to the actual 200 percent increase in Expense Budget outlays, it may be seen that the funds made available during the decade were sufficient to provide significantly better service.

Changes in City Service Levels

	Fall, 1959	Fall, 1969	Percent Increase 1959–1969
Educational enrollment			
Public schools	977,531	1,123,165	15
Higher education	85,269	172,726	103
	1960 †	1970 †	1960–1970 †
Teachers per 100 pupils	4.3	5.0	16
	1960 †	1970 †	1960–1970 †
Public aid recipients (monthly average)	321,928	1,043,606	224
	1960 †	1970 †	1960–1970 †
Monthly payment per welfare recipient	$49.84	$71.89	44
	1960 †	1970 †	1960–1970 †
Police, fire, and sanitation personnel (per 1,000 residents)	6.5	8.1	25
	1960	1969	1960–1969
Criminal complaints	410,828	1,068,897	*
	1960	1969	1960–1969
Fires	60,941	126,204	107
	1960 †	1969 †	1960–1969 †
Tonnage of waste collected	2,819,005	3,590,412	26

*A change in reporting methods makes a direct comparison improper. The increase based on consistent reporting methods is estimated at about 100 percent.

† Fiscal years.

SOURCE: The data were collected or derived from numerous reports issued by the City of New York and its departments as follows: *Executive Budget, Message of the Mayor; Annual Census of School Population;* Department of Social Services, *Monthly Statistical Report;* The City Record, *Expense Budget as Adopted;* Police Department, *Statistical Report;* Fire Department. *Annual Report;* Department of Sanitation, *Statistical Review and Progress Report;* Environmental Protection Administration, *Progress Report and Statistical Review of the Department of Sanitation.*

During the decade, enrollment in public educational institutions increased substantially more than did the population of school age. Between the school years 1959-60 and 1969-70 enrollment in public elementary and secondary day schools increased by 15 percent. Enrollment in the city's public institutions of higher education doubled, indicating a substantial increase in the number of high school graduates applying and being accepted.

During the decade, the ratio of the number of teachers per 100 pupils in the public school system rose from 4.3 to 5.0. A number of new special programs geared toward early education and promotion of opportunities for disadvantaged students were initiated, including those under Title I of the Elementary and Secondary Education Act, the More Effective Schools program, and the SEEK program under which disadvantaged high school graduates who would not otherwise qualify for entrance into the City University were enrolled and given special attention as well as certain expense allowances.

Between fiscal years 1960 and 1970, the number of public-aid recipients in the city more than tripled, although the number of "poor" families, as defined by the Social Security Administration, declined. In addition to the presumed increase in the number of female-headed families, increases in benefit levels resulted in a rise in the number of those who are eligible; there is also strong evidence that an increasing proportion of persons eligible for benefits are currently applying for welfare.[1]

Moreover, welfare recipients received higher payments than a decade ago. After adjusting for increases in living costs, the average monthly welfare payment per recipient increased by about 9 percent during the sixties, exclusive of the gains from the relatively new Food Stamp program. Thus, public aid has spread a broader net and improved the living standards of those persons eligible to receive it.

In the area of public health, the Medicaid program increased the health opportunities of low-income persons. Other programs such as neighborhood family care and maternal and infant care were initiated.

The demands upon, and activities undertaken by, city personnel

[1]A report to the House Committee on Ways and Means indicates that the numbers of families on AFDC with dead fathers, or with fathers absent because of divorce or legal separation, or where the father has deserted the family, increased by 94 percent, 37 percent, and 30 percent, respectively, between 1967 and 1968. Changes such as these within a one-year period strongly suggest that the AFDC caseload increased more rapidly than the eligible population. House Committee on Ways and Means, *Report of Findings of Special Review of Aid to Families with Dependent Children in New York City,* 91st Cong, 1st Sess., 1969.

also increased sharply in the "housekeeping" area. The number of criminal complaints received by the Police Department about doubled between 1960 and 1969; the number of fires responded to by the Fire Department more than doubled; and the tonnage of Department of Sanitation collections increased by over one-fourth. The number of uniformed city employees in these departments increased by about 25 percent.

The data indicate a sharp expansion in the proportion of persons in specific categories who have been provided with city services and also in the amount of service units provided by the city government as a whole.

REVENUES The increase in expenditures by the city is, of course, approximately matched by an increase in revenues, which also tripled during the decade. The major expansive force was intergovernmental receipts, which in 1970 stood at almost six times their 1960 level. Locally collected revenues only doubled during the period. As a share of total revenues, intergovernmental receipts rose from about one-fifth in 1960 to over two-fifths.

Receipts in the largest single category of locally collected revenue, the real estate tax, increased at a rate lower than that of the total of other locally collected receipts. The increase in real estate revenue paralleled the increase in the full valuation of taxable real estate in the city, which almost doubled. The rapid increase in real estate valuations stemmed from rapidly increasing prices of existing real estate, from a building boom in the city in the sixties as builders initiated new construction before a stricter building code was to go into effect, and also from a technical change in valuation procedure.

Total receipts from nonproperty taxes rose at a rate substantially above the rate of increase of income in the city. In large measure, this occurred as a result of the imposition of a city personal income tax in 1966. Receipts from other taxes also increased at a rate somewhat above the increase in city incomes. A change in the business tax structure in 1966 and other changes in minor taxes accounted in part for this result.

The sharp increase in intergovernmental aid received by New York City, which accounted for over half of the increase in income from all sources, resulted from a combination of factors. In part, it was due to an expansion in the number of persons eligible and applying for public services and transfer payments partially financed by state and federal funds. This was the case for welfare, where federal aid

Total Revenues: 1960–1970*

	Revenues (millions of dollars)		Percent Increase
	1960	1970	
Locally collected	*1,745*	*3,646*	*109*
Real estate taxes	979	1,893	93
Other taxes	561	1,135	102
Charges, etc.	205	618	201
Special state taxes†	—	*255*	
Intergovernmental	*481*	*2,804*	*483*
State aid	379	1,730	356
Federal aid	102	1,074	953
Total	*2,226*	*6,705*	*201*

* Fiscal years.

† Stock transfer and mortgage taxes whose receipts are turned over to the city in lieu of direct city taxation.

SOURCE: *Annual Reports of the Comptroller,* The City of New York.

is in part dependent on the number of persons receiving public assistance and where the state reimburses the city for part of the expenditures not covered by federal government payments.

Another part of the increase in intergovernmental receipts was accounted for by the liberalization of older aid programs and the development of new aid programs. The level of welfare aid per recipient under the older programs was increased over the years, as was the amount of state aid per student. A substantial increase also took place in the number of aid programs, particularly on the federal level, and in activities such as noncash aid for poor persons or poor districts. Examples of this are the Medicaid program, which finances medical outlays for low-income persons, school aid for the education of disadvantaged children, and the Model Cities Program for an attack on slum conditions.

SUMMATION In sum, the city recently experienced a number of trends that put pressure on its resources. There were changes in the age and income structure of the population which caused an increase in service requirements. Although the total population did not change significantly, an increase occurred in the demands made upon the police, fire, and sanitation departments. In addition, the wage levels of the major groups of city employees rose much more rapidly than the wages of other employees.

On the income side, the city experienced a high rate of growth of property values which permitted a rapid increase in property-tax receipts. More substantially, the city also benefited from a rapid rise in intergovernmental aid.

The sum of these trends required the city to increase its level of taxation to some degree to enable it to finance increases in service levels—more education per school-age resident; higher real levels of payments per welfare recipient; more health care for low-income persons; and a higher level of police, fire, and sanitation activities. As a result, Expense Budget outlays rose from a level equal to about 9 percent of the personal income of the city's residents in 1960 to a level equivalent to about 18 percent in 1970.

THE OUTLOOK

THE PRICE FOR CITY SERVICES

The increases in compensation secured by New York City employees during recent years have put them in a fairly favorable position. Whereas in the past it might have been valid to argue that municipal employees were underpaid, it would be difficult to argue this now.

In the cases of teachers and policemen, union leaders announced that the contracts effective in 1970 would make them among the highest-paid personnel in their respective fields in the country. Compensation provided for in these contracts appears to compare favorably with that of similarly trained and experienced people not working for local government. Furthermore, pension benefits won by the city employees are extremely liberal. City jobs competed favorably with industry jobs in nonexecutive positions, as indicated by the relative ease with which the city was able to fill its recent openings, even as the number of such openings rose as a result of newly liberalized retirement provisions.

The organization of municipal employees into unions, and the willingness of these unions not only to bargain strenuously but to undertake strikes, illegal as these may have been, has accounted in part for employee gains. Government administrators have not responded from a position of strength to union militancy, and there is no evidence that the answer is close at hand. If there is a vulnerable point in the fiscal outlook of the city, this is it.

The contracts with New York City employees in effect in 1970 were costly and added pressures to the city budget. Those negotiated with the faculties of the public schools and the city's colleges and universities provided for total increases in minimum and maximum salaries of about 20 to 40 percent over three years. These increases understate the full increase in compensation because the contracts provide for more rapid advancement toward maximum salary levels.

It is likely that labor relations between the city and its employees will remain difficult in coming years. The Citizens Budget Commission has concluded that:

> Most of the tools for sound labor relations now exist or will soon have been created. Only the Mayor can assure that they are properly used in the public interest. What is required are large doses of patience, competence and good will, an ability to understand the point of view of the other party, and the knowledge of who is who on both sides of the negotiating table.[1]

POPULATION WORKLOAD From the fiscal point of view, the age structure of New York City may be expected to change in the coming years in a more favorable manner than the change in the past decade, with the improvement concentrated in the latter half of the 1970s.[2]

The proportion of the city's population in the economically productive age group of 20 to 64 declined from 59 percent in 1960 to 57 percent in 1970. The decline is projected to bottom out in the seventies. The 0–19 year age group, responsible for the overwhelming portion of AFDC welfare aid and educational expenditures, is expected to be almost stable in relative importance through 1975 and to decline between 1975 and 1980, by contrast to its growth during the past decade.

The size of the low-income population is also relevant to the city's financial requirements. Persons living in homes without a male breadwinner constitute the largest and most rapidly growing welfare group and account for a substantial proportion of the city's other poverty-related expenditures. [The proportion of the population in such homes and receiving welfare differs sharply among ethnic groups, being high for Puerto Ricans and blacks.] Persons not born in the city also constitute a group with high welfare needs.

The influx of welfare-prone persons in the coming period may be affected by legislation presently being considered in Congress, which would set a national floor for payments to families needing public support. There is reason to expect that the bill would reduce the incentive for some potential recipients to migrate to New York City from low-welfare states. The general trend of migration of persons from Puerto Rico to the States, most of whom settle in New York, has not abated,[3] although migration slowed down in fiscal year 1971

[1] *Personnel: The Civil Service and the Municipal Unions,* The Citizens Budget Commission, 1969.

[2] Based on projections of the New York State Office of Planning Coordination.

[3] Data supplied by the Commonwealth of Puerto Rico, Department of Labor, Migration Division.

as it has at other times when the United States unemployment rate rose.

As for the other welfare categories, the size of the group of working-age persons who are physically incapable of working—the blind and the disabled—may be expected to remain stable. It also seems likely that the rate of increase in the number of old people eligible for welfare will drop, because as a group their growth rate will be lower and also because of improvements in the levels of pension benefits.

One may conclude that the rate of increase in the costs due to all anticipated changes in the age, income, and ethnic structure of the city population will not grow over the coming years, and may abate in the latter part of the decade. Taking all the cost factors into consideration, municipal expenditures are projected to rise more rapidly in dollar terms but less rapidly in percentage terms to a level of about $18 billion by 1979–80.

REVENUES—TAX RECEIPTS The rate of increase in the level of tax receipts will depend upon changes in the value of the tax base, the extent to which tax collections respond to changes in the base, and changes in tax coverage and rates.

During 1960–70, the value of taxable property in the city increased at a faster rate than the increase in incomes of residents or of employees in the city. But the increase in property values and new construction had eased by the end of the decade.

In line with national trends, the market for residential housing had become tight by 1970. However, the market for office space in the city was easing, and tax abatements on some new properties may reduce the extent to which the city property-tax collections will rise.

Studies of the relationship between changes in incomes and in real property values point to approximately equal rates of change over long periods. It would not be surprising if the future increase in taxable property values in the city were to conform to the slower rate of the late sixties rather than the faster, earlier rate.

Receipts accruing from the other tax bases of the city depend mainly on the amount of business and personal incomes. In turn, growth in each of these bases is dependent directly on the strength of the city's economy.

The overall economic pattern in New York City is one that has shown a decreasing relative importance for blue-collar activity and greater importance for white-collar activity. Some analysts have considered this a discouraging sign, suggesting that such a shift in the

	1960		1970		Percent Increase 1960–1970	
	State	Federal	State	Federal	State	Federal
Education	173	1	728	130	321	1,200
Social welfare	103	101	692	828	572	720
Other categories	31	—	48	116	55	
Noncategorical	72	—	262	—	264	
Total	379	102	1,730	1,074	356	953
Special state taxes	—	—	255			
Grand total	379	102	1,985	1,074	424	953

*Fiscal years.
SOURCE: *Annual Report of the Comptroller of the City of New York.*

economy makes it more difficult for unskilled persons to find employment. But an expansion of higher-paying, office-type employment
provides opportunities for the unskilled as well as those of high skills,
and in turn provides better opportunities for moving up the job
ladder.[1] In this respect the city's economy is in line with the national
trend, and it can only benefit from the shift toward higher-paying
and steadier employment opportunities in white-collar occupations.

Furthermore, the total employment situation in New York City
remained reasonably strong in the sixties. Over the years, the number
of jobs in the city rose at a rate somewhat above the increase in the
level of population—that is, the number of jobs available in the city
per resident increased.

There is every reason to believe that the city will participate in
future economic advances of the nation at least to the extent that it
has in the past, and perhaps more so. However, the city's economy,
like the national economy, has been subject to weakened conditions
in the beginning of the 1970s.

The restructuring of city taxes in 1966, including the imposition
of an income tax, has given the city a tax system more responsive
to changes in incomes. The progressive rates, as well as the exemp-
tions and deductions of the city personal income tax, assure that an
increasing portion of income will be taxed as incomes rise. Thus, city
income tax receipts will rise at a rate substantially exceeding increases
in total personal income in the city during the 1970s. But the level

[1] *Monthly Economic Letter,* First National City Bank, January 1970.

of revenue collections will also be more vulnerable than previously under short-term recession conditions.

REVENUES—INTERGOVERNMENTAL AID The method of determining the amount of intergovernmental funds New York City is to receive differs greatly under the respective grant-in-aid programs. Depending on the type of grant, increases in aid to be provided to the city may be more or less automatic. A substantial and growing proportion of the aid provided to the city grows automatically as the economy expands or as the city's workload and total expenditures increase. Among the major aid programs in recent years, federal participation in welfare spending was extended to cover all outlays for eligible recipients, although there had previously been a maximum dollar limitation on the federal contribution per case. The state government began to contribute about 50 percent of the cost of the City University, without an upper limit on state participation; and all the receipts of the state tax on stock transfers are now turned over to the city.

A major change in aid procedure which took effect late in the city's fiscal year 1971 was a program under which the state shares a part of its income tax collections with the city and other local governments in place of the former program of aid based on population size. However, the new state revenue-sharing program put substantial pressure on New York State's 1972 budget, which in turn resulted in a change in the aid formula that works to the disadvantage of local government.[1]

In those cases where the level of existing grants does not rise automatically as city expenditures increase, there is, of course, no guarantee that the state and federal governments will participate in the increase in city outlays in coming years as they have in the past, nor that as many new aid programs will be developed. However, there is no lack of proposals in Congress for new grant programs or for expansion of existing programs, some with excellent prospects for passage in the near future and others which have developed a momentum and may get more support in future years.

There are proposals in Congress for increased grants for health, welfare, and educational purposes and for additional grant programs in the areas of pollution control, crime control, and mass transit. Federal revenue sharing may be the eventual subject of legislation. And state aid for education, the largest single state grant program, will most likely rise in future years.

[1] The fiscal year of the state begins earlier than the fiscal year of the city.

In New York City, the approach of the time the Expense Budget is to be presented is also the approach of the time for gapsmanship. The script calls for the mayor to proclaim a "gap" between "mandatory" increases in the costs of running the city and the revenue expected in the coming fiscal year—a gap that can be closed only with a sharp increase in state and federal aid beyond that already planned in Albany and Washington. Intergovernmental aid is a substantial and growing portion of the total city budget, and it is particularly tempting to any city administration to declare bankruptcy in order to attempt to gain the maximum possible level of new aid.

It is true, however, that real problems have been created in the past by the lack of automatic increases in some major state aid programs. Because the city has been partly dependent on such funds, it has been difficult to make even "normal" increases in its budget in the absence of new state legislation. While such legislation has in the past resulted in rapid increases in aid, there was concern that it might not materialize. Such concern created an incentive to proclaim "fiscal crises" in order to improve the chances for aid-increasing legislation to be passed. This problem was temporarily abated by the state aid program permitting an automatic growth in state general aid as state income tax collections increased. However, the state revenue-sharing program, in turn, was one factor putting special pressure on the state's 1972 and 1973 budget, which required a reexamination of the level of aid that the state could provide.

The city's fiscal position is difficult. New York has traditionally been a haven for the poor and disadvantaged and cannot be expected to carry this disproportionate share of a national problem unaided. However, these burdens cannot relieve the city of the responsibility to view its total budget picture in an analytical rather than rhetorical framework.

WHAT ABOUT INFLATION? Inflation has been blamed for much of the city's fiscal woes. However, as it has boosted the cost of public services it has raised available revenues at the same time.

For example, an increase in the overall price level affects not only expenditures but also the dollar value of the city's tax base—real estate, sales, and business and personal incomes. As these bases increase in dollar amount because of a general rise in prices, real estate, business income, and sales tax collections may be expected to rise by proportionate amounts. The percentage rise in collections from the personal income tax will be greater than the increase in incomes because of the progressive nature of this levy. If the level of inter-governmental aid fails to respond to cost increases, difficulties may ensue. But until the early 1970s, the history of intergovernmental grants was that increases were more than adequate to cover the higher costs of public programs.

To be sure, costs for state and local governments rise at rates that differ from the costs for the rest of the economy. If this differential were to widen because of inflation, then it could be said that inflation damages the city's fiscal position. In fact, however, the increase in the unit cost of all state and local government purchases of goods and services in the early sixties, a period of relative price stability, averaged 1.7 percent per annum more than the increase for all goods and services, while in the relatively inflationary period in the latter half of the decade it averaged 1.8 percent.[1]

However, over a period of several years, a lag in the response of property taxes to a change in the tax base will occur because collections of property taxes are legally limited to a percentage of the average full value of taxable property for the previous five years. And, whether on a conscious or subconscious level, there is a great temptation in developing a budget during a period of rapidly rising prices to take account of the consequent buildup in tax collections on the income side of the budget but not to allow sufficient funds for increases in costs on the expenditure side. A lag in the responsiveness of property-tax collections would lead to a real lag in funds available for improvements in public programs. A lack of anticipation of the rate of increase in costs would not in itself affect the rate of improvement of service, but it would tend to raise expectations for unrealistically high rates of improvement in city services. Both factors can lead to a temporary period of budgetary tightness.

Indeed, with the bout of inflation experienced in 1970 and 1971, municipal costs were underestimated. Revenue was overestimated because the softness in business activity and in personal and business incomes which occurred was not fully anticipated in the budget calculations.

INTERGOVERNMENTAL AID AND REDISTRIBUTIVE PUBLIC PROGRAMS

There is good reason for the city administration to continue to press for the state and federal government to take over a larger share of the financial burden of welfare and welfare-related programs. A "so-

---

[1] The comparison is made by using the gross national product deflator for state and local government purchases of goods and services and the overall GNP deflator for the periods 1960–1965 and 1965–1970.

cial" policy is difficult to put into effect at any level of government, but most difficult at the local level. The greater the redistributive component of the public program, the greater are the resulting fiscal problems.

The tendency of redistributive public programs to scare off taxpayers while attracting those who benefit from such programs saps the fiscal strength of a locality—reducing the tax base while increasing the level of public service needs. This has particular relevance for the City of New York with its heavy burden of welfare and other needs associated with a large population of disadvantaged persons. However, the extent to which the city's fiscal position could be eased by greater state or federal participation is less than that implied by the welfare budget, because the city itself now provides only about one-third of such resources.

In New York City, which has a strong representation of well-to-do liberal people and poverty-stricken minority groups, there is a constant effort to redistribute economic resources. As a result, the "need" for public resources in the city will remain insatiable regardless of the level of funds flowing in.

The "need" extends beyond the direct provision of social services and transfer payments. Positions of employment with the city have been opened to "paraprofessionals," with one eye on improving the ability of city government to deliver public services and the other on opening up jobs for persons of limited skills. Changes in property zoning restrictions are frequently undertaken to assure benefits for low-income persons. Such changes reduce the potential income from property and therefore its value and tax potential. Moreover, the revenues the city can collect are limited by pressures to reduce the burden of taxes and charges for public services upon lower-income people. Tax abatements on public housing, public subsidies for transportation, and tuition-free colleges are all part of this picture.

It should be recognized that a reduction in the control of the city over its own programs is likely to follow any reduction in fiscal responsibility for these programs. If higher governments were to fully take over the financial responsibilities for the welfare program while leaving its administration completely up to the city, the welfare standards of the higher governments could not be exceeded unless the city were again willing to undertake additional financial responsibility. New York City would lack control over the relevant public programs if it were fully financed by the state or federal governments, even if the administration of the program were to remain nominally in the hands of city officials. In fact, it is to be expected that any welfare program acceptable nationally—even if fully funded by the federal government—would appear unsatisfactory in New York. The alternatives are to make do with such an "unsatisfactory" program or to return to a system under which city taxpayers bear a special burden for welfare and for other redistributive programs.

SOME OPTIONS It is correct to say that a gap exists between what the city can finance, given its current level of taxation and expected intergovernmental aid, and those public programs it would like to have.

In the public, as in the private, sector, economic resources are scarce and decisions concerning priorities must be made. Decisions must also be made concerning the relative benefits of public versus private expenditures. But the city has by no means run out of sources of potential increase in revenues. To be sure, there are political obstacles to increased tax rates and coverages and to higher charges for public services because any such increases are painful to those who must pay them. But even the receipt of intergovernmental aid cannot come about in any way except by having a government raise revenues from the private sector.

In the fiscal year 1970–71, the city increased its revenues by imposing a number of small taxes, raising its water rates and some other charges, and getting the state to cooperate in a technical change which permitted higher property tax collections within the state's constitutional limitation. Nevertheless, city tax rates on residential real estate, particularly single-family homes, are well below the rates on equivalent property in its surrounding suburbs.[1] Such underutilization of a major tax resource leads to a substantially lighter tax burden for many city residents relative to their suburban cousins, although in many cases, the city dwellers are in the higher-income brackets.

There are some good reasons for limiting reliance on the property tax. This tax tends to be less equitable than other types, and the tax burden accounted for by improvements to property is probably a drag on the upgrading of housing.

But some inequities can be reduced at the cost of increasing somewhat the complication of property or other taxes. The city could permit a credit on a part of the property taxes paid by retired persons, either against their gross property tax liability or against their city income tax liability.[2] Furthermore, the potential effect of the property

[1] See *Real Estate Taxes, Limits and Rates,* Citizens Budget Commission, 1968.
[2] Retired persons over 65 years of age with low incomes already receive favored treatment.

tax in reducing the level of new construction and modernization of older structures can be blunted by placing heavier reliance on taxation of the value of the land component of real property and by taxing the value of the improvements at a lower rate. Thus, this major tax source has the potential to be more equitable and less harmful and at the same time to bring in greater revenues than are currently being received.[1]

Nor is taxation the only source of revenue collected directly by the city that can be increased if additional funds are considered necessary. Charges for city services are also an area of potential increases. Higher education is one of the fastest increasing expenditure categories in the budget. Under the new open-enrollment program, all high-school graduates are offered higher education free of tuition (but with a low general fee), and indeed, some low-income students are currently eligible to receive expense funds (under the SEEK program). Although not unique, the university system under which there is no tuition charge for residents studying under the general day program is by no means common practice throughout the country. Even the State University of New York imposes low tuition charges. Yet, a large segment of the students at the City University can afford some payment toward the cost of their college education. A payment system could be developed which would assure that lack of funds would not be a barrier to low-income persons.

Thus, if the city desires, increases in its own collections of revenue could be secured in ways that would not adversely affect its competitive position in attracting business or make the city less attractive for middle- and upper-income residents. The illustrations presented would tend to enhance, rather than diminish, the equity of the city's taxes and charges.

If there are increases in the rate, coverage, or structure of the city revenue system in coming years, they are more likely to occur in areas of personal or business income taxation than in areas illustrated above. The opposition to increases in taxes and charges which do not involve such emotional issues as free schooling might be easier to overcome. However, the fears of the city administration that increases in personal or business income taxes might drive out business or high-income residents could have some justification.

[1]Some changes in the revenue structure might require revisions in the state constitution. These would be difficult but not impossible to secure if the city administration is determined and is supported by its voters.

New Yorkers are used to hearing each year that their city is in the midst of a fiscal crisis, that their municipal services are about to deteriorate because not enough money is available to the city government, and that the state and federal governments are to blame because they are not providing enough fiscal support.

Some years are more difficult than others. Growth in tax bases may temporarily slow down, a particularly large number of children may be about to enter school, or the growth of intergovernmental aid may not be as rapid as in previous years. More recently, New Yorkers have been bombarded by acute pressures from policemen, firemen, and other public employees for a round of "me-too" wage increases.

But over the past decade, with the city Expense Budget tripling, the evidence suggests that substantial funds were made available for use of the city government over and above that needed to pay for salary increases for city personnel and the higher costs of the things that the city must buy, and also pay for a higher level of workload needs.

The increase in funds made available permitted a large increase in city employment, in transfer payments to the needy, and in the purchase of equipment. While the scope of city activities expanded, it may be questioned whether enough attention was given to improving the quality of service available for the dollars spent.

A large part of the funds came from local revenue sources, but the most rapid proportional increase was in intergovernmental aid, which will probably continue to grow. But aid is a two-edged sword, bringing with it a growth in state and federal direct control and a corresponding dilution of the control exercised by the city. And as residents of the city are taxed by the state and federal governments to finance intergovernmental aid, the ability of the city to tap its remaining private resources is reduced.

Among the difficult jobs of the city administration is that of striking a balance between funding priority public programs from its own resources, attempting to secure intergovernmental funding for programs that aim at redistribution, and permitting citizens to retain resources in the private sector to meet their own needs. To meet such responsibilities, politicians will have to "bite the bullet" and admit to their constituents not only that public services cost money but that the money can come only from the taxpayer—whether the city gets the funds directly or otherwise.

One unfortunate effect of the idea that higher levels of government have the ability to manufacture money to fill all local government fiscal "gaps" is an overemphasis on raising the level of dollars spent for local services and an underemphasis on raising the efficiency with which these dollars are spent. When citizens are told by their government that it needs more money, they have a right to be informed also about how their government is getting the most out of the money available. But gapsmanship and crisis politics blur the recognition that resources are scarce throughout the economy and that improving efficiency is a better way than increasing expenditures to raise the level and quality of public services. In particular, those at the top level of city government must set an example by holding back on voting further salary increases such as those passed in 1969 for the New York City Council and others. Also, the city fathers will have to exercise greater courage than heretofore in effecting the economies being proposed in various professional studies currently under way.

In sum, the outlook for the future may not be completely negative. There are some signs that point to a moderate easing in the growth rate of expenditure pressures, although strains will remain. Municipal income can continue to grow, both through increases in intergovernmental aid and through increases in the city's collections of taxes and charges—if the administration and the citizens decide that new and larger programs are needed and worthwhile.

Conclusions

New York's problems—like those of other large cities—are complex, pervasive, and formidable. They are not amenable to quick solution, particularly solutions that are tied to the tenure of political administrations or promises made to gain office. But these difficulties hardly justify the general sense of fatigue and frequent expressions of despair that are reflected in the ongoing flow of rhetoric.

"Fun City" is hardly a sobriquet that fits the facts of life in New York today, but it is just as inaccurate to say that the city is in a "crisis" or—to use that most overworked of cliches—that there is a general "urban crisis." A crisis is a decisive turning point, a climacteric event that crowns a course of development. Thus, the crisis rhetoric misconstrues what is happening in New York. The city's ailments are chronic. Its state of health is like that of a person enduring the discomfort of a prolonged bout with the flu, not the pain or debilitation of a terminal illness.

Every generation is convinced that the problems confronting it are somehow unique in human experience. While the city, throughout its history, has had its share of troubles, there are facets of the contemporary urban problems which are different if not entirely new.

Rapid technological changes—both on the farm and in the factory—cause migrations of industries and people. And as a result, the central city is inundated by poor people, both black and white. Striking improvements in mass communication raise expectations of ever-

247

higher living standards and fray the patience of those who are not achieving them quickly.

One consequence is social tension. Concentrations of poor, badly educated people are a natural seedbed for group antagonisms, crime, drug abuse, and other social maladies. The political response to these phenomena is extravagant promises of simple and quick solutions to very complex problems. But these problems are deep-seated. They cannot be solved today or tomorrow. They may take several decades.

Consider, first, poverty and the administration of welfare. "Generally," it is noted in the poverty study, "an individual's welfare grants are reduced by the amount of any outside income." This means that welfare recipients are subject to a 100 percent tax whenever they try to improve their lot. It would be difficult to devise a system more deleterious to morale or more certain to create a despair that is passed on from generation to generation. Experience with a pilot program, one in which low-income families were subsidized with federal grants-in-aid, suggests that the poor will respond positively to incentives.

Housing is preeminently an area in which irrational public policies frustrate the attainment of desired goals. A distrust of market forces—a legacy of the 1930s—has kept rent control alive decades after any justification for it has disappeared. The effects are almost uniformly perverse. It protects middle-income families, not the poor. It results in the misallocation of dwelling space: A single occupant of a large apartment with a very low controlled rent has no incentive to move to a smaller one. Worst of all, rent controls—by forcing owners to abandon structurally sound buildings on which the net income, under controls, fails to cover maintenance—are shrinking New York's housing stock.

Some progress has been made since the 1930s when public policy was premised on the assumption that "decent housing" is a panacea for all social ills. Faith in that proposition led to the promiscuous use of the federal bulldozer in destroying well-established neighborhoods. It led also to construction of huge public housing complexes, such as the Pruitt-Igoe project in St. Louis which became so uninhabitable that parts of it were dynamited by order of the federal government. There are now some modest, but encouraging, signs of a change in policy, especially in the expanded system of rent supplements and housing allowances.

Other policies pursued by the city are equally vulnerable when held up to the light of reason. Under the present system, operating authorities of the mass-transit system are encouraged to treat capital as a free good, to spend freely for capital improvements while grossly undermaintaining the existing stock of equipment. Money is poured into public education programs, but there is no analysis of their effectiveness in raising intellectual levels.

It is often argued that there are no problems in New York that cannot be solved with a few more billions of dollars. Yet as documented in these pages, municipal expenditures have grown rapidly. So, too, has federal assistance, and more federal money will flow in—or back—with the enactment of some form of revenue sharing. But spending more money on misguided policies—like pouring water on flaming oil—might only make matters worse.

There is a need to reshape and reorient policies, to put the mechanisms of the marketplace to work rather than to shackle them with bureaucratic controls. Pollution exists because wastes can be dumped in the water or air at no cost to the polluter. It can be most efficiently curbed—that is, at the lowest cost to consumers who must ultimately bear the burden—by imposing charges, putting the price tags on the privilege of polluting. The same general principle, using the price system to achieve a balance between costs and benefits, can be applied to other problems that afflict New York.

Flights of crisis rhetoric sometimes end with the afterthought that "the city is really worth saving." Such affirmations are presumptuous because they imply the existence of options, of solving urban problems or somehow making cities disappear. But since most Americans live in cities or suburban areas that are linked to central city activities, there is in fact no choice at all.

The future of American cities and that of the society as a whole are inextricably tied. Progress hinges on a willingness to fashion new weapons, rational policies that offer greater hope over the long haul than any now being pursued. This book has pointed to some of them. More will have to be fashioned in the years ahead.

Credits for Photographs

Index

Index

Income taxes, New York City,
223, 234, 237, 238
negative, 42
nonresident, 225
personal, 223, 234, 237, 238
Incomes, New York City:
in ghettos, 2, 14, 29
and job training, 19, 48
for minorities, 23–25
trends in, 23
Indian Point nuclear plant,
209
Industrial firms:
exodus of, 20
and housing, 114
(*See also* Business)
Industrial-waste disposal, 186
Inflation, 227
and New York City budget
gap, 240, 241
Influx of minorities, New York
City, 14, 17, 26
(*See also* Immigration,
minority; Migration)
Institute for Development
Studies, 92
Insurance headquarters in New
York City, 11
Intergovernmental aid, 233–235,
239–243
(*See also* Federal aid; State aid)
Intermediate high schools, 79–83
International City Management
Association, 228
Inversions and air quality, 199
Investments:
ghetto, 5
housing, 99, 110–117
water-quality, 191, 192

Jacobson, Lenore, 66
Javits, Jacob K., 52
Jersey Central Railroad, 163
Job losses, 17
Job mismatches, 17–19
Job needs, 8
Job placement assistance, 88

Job training:
and business, 5, 48
and income level, 19, 48
and school system, 48
Jobs, New York City, 4, 10,
17–19, 222, 238
and better housing, 129
for the disadvantaged, 42
and education, 19
and ghetto unemployed, 18,
19, 26, 30
and mass transit, 179
and minority groups, 18, 26
openings for, by type, 3, 4,
11, 17–19, 237
suburban, 10
trends in, 17–21

Kansas City, Missouri, air
control, 185
Kennedy, Senator Robert F., 46
Kennedy International Airport,
access to, 152, 153, 163
Kindergarten, 91

Labor and mass transit, 172
Labor productivity and poverty,
55, 56
Laborer jobs, 17–19
Lake Towers apartment in
Chicago, 122
Landfill:
offshore, 213, 214
and solid-waste disposal, 213
Large families and welfare, 35,
36
Lateness, cost of, 134
Learning problems, 83
Limited Profit Companies, New
York State, 110
Lindsay, Mayor John V., 1
Living costs in New York City,
23
Local Law 14, 211, 212
London rapid transit, 136
Long Island, commuters from,
133